PRAISE FOR LEO ROMERO

"Now, here we are, with a classic collection, by one of the most import-
ant poets of his time and place. Stop and listen to the remembered
dream of a generation, a life, the edge of a flowering desert in time."

—JOY HARJO, from the foreword

"Leo Romero—a poet of short line, scenes of daily life, sun, mountain,
tree, and moon in northern New Mexico—stands singular. Dreams
come to life when you listen to the roots, notice leaves, seeds, and
the movement of all beings, things, underground and above. A most
valuable text, illuminating and embracing moments rarely spoken or
revealed."

—JUAN FELIPE HERRERA, emeritus poet laureate of the United
States and author of *Half of the World in Light: New and Selected Poems*

"Poetry is ageless because of time. Memory is back when, and today
is now. Time is both past and present. Decades ago are decades later.
Time is still ageless, more or less. I met Leo in the late 1960s. . . . And
I vividly remember telling myself: this young Chicano guy Romero is
a poet and a soothsayer. Watch out. And he was and is."

—SIMON J. ORTIZ, author of *Light As Light*

"A luminous journey across a life of poetry, Leo Romero offers a
profound work full of life, communion, and connection to land and
community."

—SANTIAGO VAQUERA-VÁSQUEZ, author of *Nocturno de frontera*

"*Trees Dream of Water* is a captivating ride through memory, identity,
and life in northern New Mexico. Leo Romero's mastery of language
and deep connection to his heritage shines through in every poem.
The poems are deeply personal and universally resonant. This is a
must-read for anyone interested in the intersection of culture, nature,
and the art of poetry. This book is a must-read for anyone seeking to
understand loss and the search for belonging."

—RUBEN QUESADA, author of *Brutal Companion*

"Deeply rooted in New Mexico, Leo Romero's poems are honed to simplicity and transform situations and narratives into myth. Following no trend but staying true to his inner compass, Leo Romero has created a poetry that is humble, moving, and thrilling to the core."

—ARTHUR SZE, author of *The Glass Constellation:*
New and Collected Poems

"Listening to Leo Romero's story-anecdote-half-whispered poems can be like breaking into an old-fashioned rural phone party line and catching soulful fragments pulled from the deepest melancholy of this haggard region. Impeccably modest, conversationally incomplete, painfully personal, sometimes his unpretentious glimpses of family, friends, the intimacies of mountain hamlet life, carry an authenticity I have never experienced in words before. Born of an almost forgotten northern New Mexican experience, they are akin to magic, they are how Chicano history might actually sound were it allowed to speak for itself. Leo Romero is the region's living treasure."

—PETER NABOKOV, author of *Where the Lightning Strikes:*
The Lives of American Indian Sacred Places

"In this moving retrospective, Romero's poems take us into the rural Southwest—its people, flora and fauna, indelible landscapes. Whether the perspective is from the poet-self or a persona, the journey is deep and lonesome, forged by history and ancestry, reflected in the 'the throbbing / of the mountains / The slow breathing of trees . . . the uneasiness / of the fields.'"

—VALERIE MARTÍNEZ, author of *Count*

TREES DREAM OF WATER

Trees Dream of Water

Selected and New Poems

LEO ROMERO

THE UNIVERSITY OF
ARIZONA PRESS

TUCSON

The University of Arizona Press
www.uapress.arizona.edu

We respectfully acknowledge the University of Arizona is on the land and territories of Indigenous peoples. Today, Arizona is home to twenty-two federally recognized tribes, with Tucson being home to the O'odham and the Yaqui. Committed to diversity and inclusion, the University strives to build sustainable relationships with sovereign Native Nations and Indigenous communities through education offerings, partnerships, and community service.

ISBN-13: 978-0-8165-5422-5 (paperback)
ISBN-13: 978-0-8165-5423-2 (ebook)

Cover design by Leigh McDonald
Cover art by Leo Romero, photographed by Elizabeth Cook Romero
Designed and typeset by Leigh McDonald in Warnock Pro 10.5/14 and Meridien (display)

Publication of this book is made possible in part by the proceeds of a permanent endowment created with the assistance of a Challenge Grant from the National Endowment for the Humanities, a federal agency.

Library of Congress Cataloging-in-Publication Data
Names: Romero, Leo, author.
Title: Trees dream of water : selected and new poems / Leo Romero.
Description: [Tucson] : University of Arizona Press, 2025. | Series: Camino del sol: a Latinx literary series
Identifiers: LCCN 2024009746 (print) | LCCN 2024009747 (ebook) | ISBN 9780816554225 (paperback) | ISBN 9780816554232 (ebook)
Subjects: LCGFT: Poetry.
Classification: LCC PS3568.O5644 T74 2025 (print) | LCC PS3568.O5644 (ebook) | DDC 811/.54—dc23/eng/20240617
LC record available at https://lccn.loc.gov/2024009746
LC ebook record available at https://lccn.loc.gov/2024009747

Printed in the United States of America
♾ This paper meets the requirements of ANSI/NISO Z39.48-1992 (Permanence of Paper).

for

Elizabeth

(since 1979 in Taos)

CONTENTS

AGUA NEGRA (1981)

CELSO (1980) (1985)

GOING HOME AWAY INDIAN (1990)

SAN FERNANDEZ BEAT (1992)

BEYOND NAGEEZI

1.

2.

3.

FOREWORD

AN EARLY MEMORY, or was it a dream, that comes to mind when I think back to Thanksgiving 1971: I was an undergraduate at the University of New Mexico, majoring in studio art, living in a small student rental house slapped down behind a duplex that faced Coal Avenue, not far from Yale Boulevard. The day before, I had been refused food stamps because my tuition and book money, which counted as income, disqualified me. I couldn't afford to buy traditional holiday fare and was concerned because I had invited the poet Leo Romero to spend Thanksgiving dinner with me, my toddler son, and my then partner, the Acoma poet Simon J. Ortiz. Ortiz had been Romero's mentor a year earlier in the Upward Bound Program and had encouraged his poetry. Romero visited us frequently and we'd sit around the table and talk politics, art, and poetry, our favorite subjects. He didn't have any place to go in Albuquerque for the holiday. I didn't ask but he contributed ten dollars for dinner. I don't know if he remembers, and I'm sure I did not tell him, but because of him I was able to buy a turkey, some milk for gravy, and cranberry sauce. I had everything else for corn bread dressing, green beans, and potatoes. Because of him, we had a traditional Thanksgiving dinner. And by the way, as Native people, we didn't celebrate the coming of the Puritans. We celebrated having food to eat.

Romero was one of the first "real" poets I met, after Ortiz. I was intrigued. I loved poetry but had always assumed poets were far away in time and place, nowhere near my home or tribal nation, until I went to the Institute of American Indian Arts, which, in 1967, was a Bureau of Indian Affairs boarding school for young Native artists.

There was a poetry anthology published and paid for every year by the actor Vincent Price, featuring the work of student poets from many different places, many tribal nations. Romero and Ortiz were serious poets. Ortiz had publications and a book coming out. Romero was also publishing and writing a book.

Romero in those younger years was the same as he is now, in that he was self-possessed, inquisitive, and knowledgeable on not just literary matters. He also demonstrated quite an incredible memory for detail. When I walked into his bookstore on Cerrillos Road in Santa Fe, a few years before COVID-19 struck, and we caught up, he surprised me with details he remembered from those times in the early seventies when we made our way as young poets in the literary community, doing readings, going to workshops, and taking part in other cultural events. His memory acted as a spark to my memory.

Romero and I met just as I had begun writing my own poems. I had been given a copy of Pablo Neruda's collection *The Captain's Verses* and was struck by Neruda's lyric eloquence, much like what captivated me in Romero's and Ortiz's poetry. Their poems spoke in the language of the everyday, lifted up a little so you could see the trees and rivers, and hear the animals stirring in the grass, the birds, the lover in the other room getting ready to open the door. What gave tension was the unspoken, which could be the growling hunger of poverty, the echo of war, the crying out of grief—some of it centuries old.

As we recalled those years we knew each other as young poets, I noted what a cultural literary shift had been happening at that time in New Mexico. Native (we were "American Indian" then) poets and writers like Ortiz, Leslie Marmon Silko, and N. Scott Momaday were forerunners of what became known as the Native American Renaissance, a flourishing alongside the explosion of Chicano literature, thought, and culture, which was celebrated through the Festival Floricanto events organized by the Chicano poet Alurista. Celebratory readings and events took place from California to Texas, including New Mexico, touting the fierce wave of Chicano poets, including Alurista, Lorna Dee Cervantes, and Leroy V. Quintana. I remember the giant presence of Ricardo Sánchez, who proclaimed that poetry was wherever we all landed in our reveries. Leslie Silko was hired as a visiting writer at the university and brought African American novelist and culturalist Ishmael Reed to speak. He was a kind of literary warrior, questioning the canon of American literature, asking why American literature excluded all voices, all cultures. He also pulled together historic gatherings of multicultural readings that included a diversity of American voices, many who would later become known as essential to the now-broken-open literary canon. These cultural literary events were not well received by the canon keepers.

Across from campus, the Living Batch Bookstore had become an essential stop for poets and writers coming through who wanted to promote new work, peruse the newest publications, or just hang out with the community. The University of New Mexico's reading series included risk takers and essential voices like Anne Waldman, Galway Kinnell, and Ai.

This was the atmosphere in which Leo Romero emerged as a young Hispanic, or Spanish New Mexico, poet. There were many discussions in the Hispanic literary communities in New Mexico about the term "Chicano," which acknowledged native cultural roots from Mexico and considered whether it included the "Spanish" of northern New Mexico, the place of Romero's Chacón home. These political crosswinds were fanning across the country, with the feminist movement picking up, especially among Anglo women, the ongoing Vietnam War protests, and the emerging sovereignty of Native nations. The fight for equality for African Americans in all areas of life was afire too, fed by regenerative and creative thinking offered in fresh literature. As young poets, we realized that our poetry could not help but be political; to speak and write, after all we had been through culturally, was to find a place to thrive, to be remembered and dreamed by those who would come after.

I first read Leo Romero's poetry in pages, in drafts. They were typed by typewriter on white paper and handed to me to read. Each of those early poems was rooted in the mythic, earthic realm of that hometown village of Chacón where Romero was born and went back to, either physically or in dreams. Each poem was rooted in natural imagery. Yet consider that every poet writes of the natural world. There could be no poetry without seasons, animals, plants, birds, geographical places, or weather. Every poem is situated somewhere, even in the imagination. And even the imagination is not without seasons, animals, plants, birds, geographical places, or weather. Romero's poems are the essence of northern New Mexico, influenced even subtly by the local Native Pueblo cultures—as illustrated in "Way of the Falling Rain":

Overhead clouds are becoming mountains
The rain is silent as the deer
The rain is running like frightened deer
The cicadas have changed into men
Waving green branches and beating the ground
Men without voices and copper bells
This is the way of the falling rain

I can't help but think of Rudy Anaya and his groundbreaking novel *Bless Me, Ultima*, first published in 1972, and how much it was in and of the northern New Mexico culture, then in the early seventies and even now. The magic of earth medicine knowers was often viewed as a kind of magical realism by those outside the cultural experience, even as those in practice and culture knew it to exist in ordinary reality. It's a grounded reality. We see how what is called "magical realism" is ever present in Romero's poems, often expressed in the literary technique of surrealism.

In the time of *Bless Me, Ultima*, in the time of the collective coming-of-age of cultural diversity in this country, there were no cell phones, there were no computers, no internet, no massive communication portals like the various social media stores that crowd our mind waves for attention, for now. The number of likes didn't determine the value of a poet, a writer. The poetry in *Trees Dream of Water: Poems Selected and New* takes us to a place, a kind of country of alert attention. We must stop for magic to happen, to see it, to recognize it, to know it. Poetry is a kind of elixir of words in which the rain, deer, cicadas, trees, dancers bringing rain exist in the voice, the breath of the speaker, the poet who says, *I am here / we are here and because these words exist and they sing, we are a remembered dream.*

When I walked into Romero's bookstore all these years later, I asked him, as I used to when we were young, "What are you working on? Are you still writing?" He said, "Yes. I have manuscripts. But I haven't sent anything for publication in a long time. I lost interest in publishing, but I've kept writing." Now, here we are, with a classic collection, by one of the most important poets of his time and place. Stop, and listen to the remembered dream of a generation, a life, the edge of a flowering desert in time.

—*Joy Harjo, Muscogee Nation reservation, August 9, 2023*

INTRODUCTION

A FEW YEARS AGO, Joy Harjo was completing her term as the twenty-third poet laureate of the United States. She is the first Native American poet to hold this honor. As poet laureate, Harjo's principal project was called "Living Nations, Living Words," which highlighted Native nation poets through an interactive story map and an audio collection. There are poets adjacent to Native American writers, however, whom she admires, whom she considers part of her creative community and worthy of championing also. One of them is Leo Romero, whom she first met in 1970 through Simon J. Ortiz, Romero's then undergraduate counselor at the University of New Mexico.

Harjo dropped by Romero's bookstore in Santa Fe, and during their conversation, she inquired why he had stopped publishing. He clarified that though it was true it had been some time since his last publication, he *had* been writing all this time. He hadn't lost his passion for poetry; it was the business of pursuing a publisher that didn't interest him anymore. Harjo convinced Romero that he needed to do right by his creative gift and offered to assist in finding a publisher for his next book. Where did he imagine placing it? Romero felt that Camino del Sol might be a good home for *Beyond Nageezi*. It was then that Harjo approached the University of Arizona Press.

The name Leo Romero was not new to me. For the Chicano literary community, Romero is one of our foundational poets whose work is situated primarily in New Mexico, speaking to a landscape and way of life that has been steadily diminishing as the state's economic priorities shift from the rural to the industrial. He keeps solid company with other Chicano poetry legends of his generation: Alurista, Juan Felipe Herrera, Gary Soto, Luis Omar Salinas, Leroy V. Quintana, Jimmy Santiago Baca, and Carmen Tafolla, to name a few. Like the creative work of these poets, Romero's poems have a reach that spans across his home state and beyond, providing remarkable insights into the Southwest's past and present. But unique to his poetry is its exploratory temperament—the search for the self in a vast natural environment that could also be overwhelmingly isolating. In his own words, "For me writing poetry was a matter of survival. It gave meaning to the world that otherwise could seem meaningless. Through the struggles and setbacks I had as a young man I could always pause and reflect and sometimes make poetry of my experiences. Poetry grounded me, allowed me to see life in a greater perspective, not just my limited self. Through poetry, I felt connected to what matters: existence."

Romero's last book of poetry was published in 1992, thus I was thrilled to know that he was still writing and still guiding us through the wondrous Land of Enchantment. It wasn't enough to publish his latest collection of poems, however; Romero deserved a more fitting acknowledgment. And so the idea was born to produce a more substantive representation of his oeuvre through the shaping of a selected and new volume of poems—a prominent marker of a notable person of letters.

It has been such an honor to revisit the body of work of a poet who encounters nature in all its beauty and complexity. But for those who are not familiar with Romero, the following biographical sketch and subsequent analytical reading of his poetry will be useful. And I hope readers of this long-overdue collection will be as taken by Romero's poetry as I have been since I first encountered it as a graduate student in the mid-1990s, when I was hungry for literary mentors and poems that exercised the directness of language and the discipline of compression to tell a grand and compelling story.

The state of New Mexico is home to the largest Latino population in the United States and home to the second-largest Native American population, outnumbered only by Alaska. Its deeply rooted Spanish and Indigenous ancestry is reflected in the state flag, which bears a

Pueblo people's ancient sun symbol, the Zia, over the same gold that radiates from the flag of Spain. In 1912, it became the forty-seventh state of the Union; since then, New Mexico's multicultural identity has flourished, due to its robust ethnic demographic. Other relevant particulars: New Mexico has one of the most diverse geographical landscapes, and each year it consistently ranks as one of the poorest states in the nation. These details open an important window into the work of its creative artists, such as Leo Romero, whose poetry is shaped by an intimate knowledge of New Mexico's land and its people.

Romero was born on September 25, 1950, in his grandparents' house, which stood near the unincorporated community of Chacón. Once Comanche territory, it was rumored that the land where his grandparents lived was at one time called Los Romeros, or Romero-ville, reflecting the surname of the largest family of inhabitants. Located east of the Sangre de Cristo Mountains, and at that time one of several sparsely populated villages in Mora County, Chacón has the distinction of being named after its first postmaster, a common practice in small northern New Mexico towns.

Romero's mother, Ortencia, was one of the oldest of a dozen children. And though her parents owned a cattle farm, it was a small-scale operation, not enough to sustain such a sizable household. As the children became adults, many left to seek employment elsewhere. Several relocated to California's Bay Area, but Ortencia, newly married, moved to Santa Fe, and then Flagstaff, Arizona, and eventually Las Vegas, New Mexico, after fleeing, with her three children in tow, an abusive marriage. After Ortencia became pregnant by a younger man, she decided to bear her child in Chacón. And because she was a single mother, she gave her fourth child her maiden name. His father's identity would remain unknown to Romero until well into adulthood. And since his half siblings were seven to ten years older than he was, Romero grew up like an only child while witnessing his family contend with financial hardship.

At a few months old, Romero moved with his immediate family back to Las Vegas, which paled in comparison to Chacón's natural beauty. It was in this new town that Romero began to transition to speaking mostly in English, which made communication with his Spanish-speaking grandparents difficult, although his visits to Chacón were rare because his mother didn't own a car, nor did she know how to drive. Those visits, however, were impressive enough to inspire Romero's early poems.

Those early poems were written in 1969, while Romero was an undergraduate at the University of New Mexico in Albuquerque via the Upward Bound Program, an enrollment that kept him from becoming drafted into the war in Vietnam. There, he befriended his Upward Bound counselor Simon J. Ortiz, enrolled member of the Pueblo of Acoma. A graduate of the International Writing Program at the University of Iowa, Ortiz encouraged Romero to pursue a master's degree in English at New Mexico State University in Las Cruces, which Romero began in 1974. During this period, he also served as the editor of New Mexico State's literary magazine *Puerto del Sol*. But after a year in graduate school, Romero began to feel stifled by academia and disenchanted with the poetry he was producing, so he returned to Chacón to breathe new life into his childhood memories and the stories he had been told by his grandparents. Indeed, in Chacón he began to absorb the world of his family and ancestors, connecting with his grandmother on a level he had not experienced before. This trip home energized his creativity, and when he returned to complete his second year of graduate school, Romero produced a high volume of poetry invoking Chacón and his loved ones. But one semester later, presented with the opportunity of a full-time job, he dropped out of college to start earning a living.

After several stints in such places as the Social Security Administration in Clovis and the Bernalillo County Mental Health Center, Romero decided to return to New Mexico State to complete his degree in 1981, six years after leaving the master's program. If he didn't complete that degree now, he reasoned, he never would. And a few years later, he made the risky but life-changing decision to make a living as a bookseller. He has been owning and running no fewer than five bookstores, at different times, since 1988. His wife, Elizabeth Cook-Romero, has been his partner in three of the bookstores. Currently, they manage Books of Interest in Santa Fe, New Mexico. It was during his time as a bookseller, surrounded by books and engaging book-buying customers, that he published almost half of his body of work with various small presses, enriching the New Mexico and Chicano poetry canons.

A note about Romero's use of the word *Indian*: in today's sensitive approach to ethnic identities, such a word has become anathema if spoken or written by a non–Native American. Romero, however, is a poet of his time, and therefore employs the nomenclature of his time, when such usage was commonplace, particularly in places where Native American populations thrived, like New Mexico. As a Californian who moved to Arizona and then New Mexico in the mid-1990s, I was surprised at how often I'd encounter this word on the streets or in spoken-word performances, without any pejorative undertones. This did not give me permission to use it, but it did allow me to accept that in these communities, the word existed and was expressed freely, and did not carry the same political charge that it did in the classrooms of academia. For the sake of preserving the voice and lexicon of the original poems, I opted not to censor that word in Romero's work. To do otherwise would be disingenuous, applying a practice that was not part of the editorial vetting for small presses until recently. It is critical, however, that I address its use because those who will hold this book in their hands will be readers of *this* time.

In his two earliest books, *During the Growing Season* and *Agua Negra*, Romero establishes his stylistic choices and the process of world making. Readers will notice that he typically doesn't punctuate the ends of sentences, gesturing toward an open-endedness or a story in medias res. Though each poem functions with a beginning and an end, the goal is not to offer an experience or observation as a self-contained unit but as part of a lengthier narrative. Though several poems speak to a moment or event recalled as a single memory or reflection, collectively they piece together a portrait of a dynamic interior life. Since the poems lean toward the autobiographical, that life is the poet's. Poetic license, however, doesn't bind the poet to objective fact, but it does allow the conceit of subjective or even selective recollection. Punctuation is more prominent and practical when there is dialogue—to distinguish between the speaker's voice and those of the various characters that populate the poems.

The title and opening line in Romero's poems tend to be identical—an echo that keeps the energy of the language tranquil and restrained. The short line lengths and the capitalization of the first word of each sentence also serve a pragmatic purpose: to avoid confusing or ambiguous readings. These features also control the rhythmic beat of the poem. To match the pensive tone, the lines favor the simple sentence structure, rarely resort to pauses or caesuras, and tend to break on clauses:

> *But weeds grew everywhere*
> *and I spent hours*
> *pulling them*
> *Yet for all that work*
> *the frost killed everything*
> *By mid-August*
> *all the corn plants were dead*
> *For many days after*
> *I would spend hours*
> *among the dried corn*
> *watching and thinking*
> *how they were like stiff ghosts*

The succinctness of the poems, however, belies that vastness of the setting being summoned with common nouns. In the excerpt above, "weeds" and "corn." In others, "valley," "mountains," "river," "soil," "fields," "forest," and "moon." The merging of the wild with the domestic is demonstrated by the sentient beings that coexist in this space: deer and cicadas appear alongside horses and chickens. Here, birds sing, but so do the women washing clothes at the river.

The world Romero builds offers a rich sensory experience. Certainly visual and tactile, but he's most closely attuned to the auditory. These noises, however, are not mysterious or ominous but distinctly identifiable, which can be comfortingly familiar at best; at worst, sleep depriving: "I hear the mare neigh / for the fiftieth time"; "Last night frightened wings / kept me awake"; "This late at night / you listen to the chickens."

In a community that depends on the seasons, the harvest, and the health of farm animals to secure survival, if not livelihood, one element stands out: the rain. In Chacón, the rain is a bittersweet visitor. It nurtures the forests and crops, but it also brings with it a melancholy memory: the death of the speaker's grandfather. Rain sounds like grief, and at age ten, the speaker came to understand mortality. Even though the boy cannot speak much Spanish, nor the grandfather much English, the two intersect in a house that witnesses a beginning and an end: "The house where I was born / Where my grandfather was dying / of prostate cancer." And to acknowledge the Indigenous essence of the land, Romero describes rain clouds "appearing like smoke signals." Falling rain evokes "A moving of feet and shaking rattles / Necklaces of corn and turquoise swaying."

There are two significant developments in *During the Growing Season*. The first is the introduction of a figure who will become the main protagonist in one of Romero's future books: Celso. This character is a trickster, storyteller, and picaro (as in a picaresque narrative), and more will be said in the discussion of the poetry book titled with Celso's name.

The second is the portraiture of the speaker as a young man who, despite his affection for his ancestral land and family, yearns for change, likely disaffected by his current circumstances, moving from one place to another in search of something else. Employment? Adventure? Independence? It's not clear whether he's running away from anyone or anything, but he's in a constant state of movement. No poem exemplifies this better than in the epistolary poem "Letter to Erlinda," in which a possible romance brews with the woman of "Yaqui blood." Erlinda becomes a confidant, the person to whom he reports via correspondence the various destinations of his journey— from New Mexico to Texas to Colorado and Nebraska and beyond. In the subsequent poem "Hitchhiking," the speaker reveals that he's traveling with very low funds but at maximum energy:

I hitchhike
in this great land
with America screaming
in my ears
With its nose turned up at me
With me
alone
My body bursting with life

The speaker moves through Iowa and Missouri, eventually getting dropped off in Kansas City, where he contemplates reaching out to Erlinda but decides to postpone communication until he's closer to home. So too is the possibility of matrimony suspended:

> *You want to have*
> *ten children you told me*
> *But how can I support you*
> *and children?*
>
> *When I'm barely getting by*
> *going to college*
> *And no car*
> *That's always an issue*

This shift from the sometimes sentimental memories of the past to the harsh realities of the speaker's present is not as incongruous as it might seem. A clearer profile of the speaker's difficult childhood unfolds in Agua Negra, a ghost town located close to Chacón. In the heartbreaking poem "One Day Before Christmas," the speaker and his mother (who is raising her son on her own) stand in the food line. And when that food runs out, they "would get / reacquainted / with what it was like / to starve." It's no wonder that, in an earlier poem, the speaker states, "I couldn't wait to leave home / when I graduated from high school / ten years ago / and left for Albuquerque / in a matter of days." We learn that the mother purchases an icebox on credit. It didn't run on electricity, requiring a block of ice; it was the mother's hard-won effort to bring some hope into the home. And though the speaker is back on the road in the poem "Artificial Flowers," he carries his childhood and the memories of his mother with him, signaling that he's not necessarily escaping but looking for opportunities to better himself, in honor of his mother's sacrifices. He holds no ill will toward her or their poverty. He remembers her lovingly, noting:

> *I think of my mother when*
> *she was young*
> *and think of how*
> *beautiful*
> *and strong*
> *she was*
> *I think of her*
> *now old*
> *and think how*
> *she's still beautiful*

If *During the Growing Season* doesn't dwell on the speaker's intent in revisiting places and people of times past, *Agua Negra* certainly underscores it. He's motivated by a desire to understand where he comes from and learn who these people were who played such important roles in his formative years. At the very least, knowing these facts offers a kind of comfort for the speaker. But he's quite aware that it will be no easy task: "I search for a history of this valley / but no one wrote it down / so I look for anything." He's met with the challenge that "most of the people / have died / or moved away," so he relies on the memory of those intimate moments with his mother and grandparents to fill in those absences and silences. What the reader comes to appreciate is that the speaker comes from a place of struggle, though not without love. Returning to his origins is one way to make peace with the past, and to forgive himself for leaving, though that departure was unavoidable.

With Celso, Romero adds an intriguing religious dimension to his poems that was not present in the previous two books, whose emotional movements are akin to spiritual journeys. Like the previous speaker, Celso's family roots run deep in the community of Agua Negra. And like the previous speaker, Celso's father is completely absent, though Celso is more explicit about that heartache because the townspeople keep asking him about his father, a passive-aggressive method of broadcasting his perceived illegitimacy. (Though a father and a mother are mentioned in a poem, soon after Celso's birth the mother dies and the father vanishes, leaving a "spinster aunt" to raise him as her own. The implication here—and one that the townspeople seem to be gesturing at—is that the aunt is the unwed mother.) It's not until he becomes an adult that he comes up with a stinging response that strikes at the heart of the town's Catholic values:

> *But when Celso became a man*
> *and people would ask him*
> *who his father was*
> *He would answer them bluntly*
> *that he was the product*
> *of an immaculate conception*
> *just like Jesus*

but that he had no great plans
for the salvation of mankind

And damn if he'd die
on a cross
for their sins

This sacrilegious bravado has been a lifetime in the making, though Celso's early relationship to Catholicism is a positive one. Once, after confession, he feels particularly blessed: "And when I walked out of the church / the world was different / Clearer, a little like heaven." The moon, he declares, is his personal guardian angel. As a clever young man, he reasons that when the priest drowned in the river, the water became holy, inspiring his entrepreneurial spirit—he sells it for "50 CENTS A BUCKETFUL." When he sees the face of Jesus on a wall of a house, the news travels fast and people from faraway places come to witness this miracle. Celso secures his reputation as the town mystic, but also the class clown, a dual identity that collapses into one when he succumbs to his vice.

Celso the alcoholic tells tall tales that are tinged with enough religious belief to engage his listeners, like his claim that he pulled three long strands of hair from the head of his guardian angel when Celso caught him sleeping on the job. When Celso's drunk, he's more than happy to flaunt them. Intoxicated, he screams out the window to plead with the dead to cease their "drunken merriment"—the clacking of their bones keeps him up. Besides being able to hear and see the dead, Celso perceives the Sorrowful Madonna in Josefita, a young widow. The biblical figure Job comes to him in a dream. They drink together and exchange complaints about their burdens. Celso does not fabricate for the sake of deceit, and it would be too easy to dismiss his claims as the rantings of a drunk. Yet he understands his contribution to the community and that the townspeople are more than willing to listen because he's both sage and buffoon, a spiritual guide and an entertainer. The weight of this responsibility, however, is exhausting, and after bearing it for six decades, Celso, gray haired, unmarried, and childless, sheds both identities by becoming sober. In this clearheaded state, he must now face the difficult truth of who he really is.

If there is any doubt about Celso's lifelong function in that town, the speaker removes it when he steps out of the shadows to consult with Celso about a very personal matter. Feeling unmoored and unsure about his own purpose in life, he entreats Celso in earnest:

> *Celso, look at me honestly*
> *and tell me*
> *what it is that you see*
> *I ask but I am afraid to know*
>
> *Does it matter that I was born*
> *and that I have lived this long*
> *And all for what*
> *Has it been a waste,*
> *my life*
> *Can a life such as mine*
> *have mattered*

Celso's redeeming qualities eventually eclipse his flaws, which is a grand statement to make about people who live in ordinary working-class towns but whose lives bear deep meaning. This is the backbone and foundation of Romero's poetics.

In a conversation with me, Romero revealed that *Going Home Away Indian* is inspired by his friendships with Simon J. Ortiz and Joy Harjo, and by the sense of displacement he witnessed in Indigenous men separated from their homes and families, something he could relate to: "There were a lot of urban Native Americans in Albuquerque at the time, and I thought of the dilemma they were under. They longed for home but when they returned it was no longer home, so they came back to Albuquerque. It was like me growing up in a barrio in Las Vegas where I had been disconnected from my source." Another important influence was a book of paintings by the groundbreaking Native American artist Fritz Scholder, who is credited with redefining the depictions of Native American people in art: "I would open the book at random, look at a painting, get a charge from that painting, which would lead to a poem. As I looked at the paintings, I would remember Simon, I would remember Joy, and the [Native American] students who were in the Upward Bound Program [with me]." For more background on the book's title and further context on the creation of the poems within, please see Romero's note at the end of the selections from *Going Home Away Indian*.

Though Romero alludes to tensions between Native American and Mexican communities, he focuses instead on the love triangle between Raymundo, a Mexican poet; "Skeleton Indian"; and Skeleton's beloved "Marilyn Monroe Indian," who had "a movie star / look about her." Through Skeleton's eyes, Raymundo learns about the plight of Native Americans, the sense of dislocation endured when they leave the reservations and struggle to adapt to urban spaces, which could be hostile and discriminatory against Indigenous people. But Skeleton, despite his homesickness, is perceived as a success story by those who notice his self-assured walk and demeanor:

> *he's the talk*
> *of the town*
> *from hogan*
> *to Pueblo*
> *to tepee*
> *to apartment complex*
> *in Albuquerque's*
> *SE Heights*
> *Skeleton Indian*
> *he's the talk*
> *of the town*
> *in his turquoise colored*
> *boots*
> *and Arrow shirts*
> *This is no*
> *government Indian*
> *He's an escaped*
> *Indian*
> *No reservation*
> *can hold him*
> *for long*

Despite this confidence, Skeleton is haunted by nightmares depicting atrocities of times past, 1856 to be exact, when a Native American forefather is shot by a white man on a train who is aiming at a buffalo. That death by gunshot to the head plays out on several occasions in his dreams.

Another poignant poem, "That's John Colley," references the life-altering decisions the American government made on behalf of Native Americans. John Colley is John Collier, the well-meaning reformer of federal policies toward Native Americans. He thought of himself as an advocate for Native American self-rule and the preservation of Native American culture, but some of his policy proposals, like the termination of the land allotment system, were not that popular with the communities he was serving. Though John Collier passed away in 1968, he is remembered still, and not in a flattering light: "The damage's done."

The meeting between Skeleton and Raymundo is fraught at first, but eventually they become friends, drinking buddies, both smitten by the same woman. But it's the fact that Raymundo's a poet that leads to his demise, as per Skeleton's realization:

> *I didn't know*
> *he was so afflicted*
> *Poetry must have*
> *killed him*
> *You really think so*
> *Marilyn frowns*
> *I should have discouraged*
> *him*
> *from writing me all*
> *those love poems*
> *They must have*
> *taxed*
> *his heart*

Raymundo's death is attributed to his creativity and ability to see the world differently than the average human being. He becomes lost in the realm of the dead, much like Mictlán, the underworld in pre-Columbian mythology. It is on this plane that he's able to fully connect with Skeleton and Marilyn Monroe, who are surprised to find him there because they "thought this reservation / was only for Indians." This is a compelling reunion because, being Mexican, Raymundo does indeed have Amerindian ancestry, but it takes them time to comprehend that. It's not until they move past arguing over whose fault it is that they're stuck together for all eternity that they are able to recognize their commonality. By healing one rift between Mexicans and Native Americans, they're able to find peace.

As previously mentioned, several of Romero's maternal aunts and uncles moved to the Bay Area, San Francisco in particular, to make a living. This exodus from the family land was not something Romero dwelled on since it was strictly a financial decision. San Francisco, however, was in his mind for an entirely different reason: that was one of the places closely associated with the Beats, an influential literary generation Romero gravitated toward as a young reader, and which had its heyday in the 1950s, about the time that Romero's relatives relocated to the West Coast. These two worlds collided for Romero when he came upon a book of photographs by Ira Nowinski called *Cafe Society: Photographs and Poetry from San Francisco's North Beach*, depicting the local establishments that such figures as Lawrence Ferlinghetti and Allen Ginsberg popularized as bohemian havens. In one of those photographs, Romero recognized his uncle Margarito inside a cigar store. Suddenly, a movement that was stewarded by mostly white and some African American poets acquired a Latino dimension for Romero, inspiring *San Fernandez Beat*.

This book is somewhat of an outlier in Romero's body of work. Perhaps that's why he chose to employ punctuation at the end of sentences—a feature excluded in his previous books. There's also the humorous angle, inevitable because Romero considers *San Fernandez Beat* a parody, written not maliciously but in the spirit of tragicomedy. Unlike the famous Beats of San Francisco, Alfred Martinez is the unheralded poet of San Fernandez who, to cultivate a literary reputation, changes his name to A. Ginsberg. He explains, "Do you think anyone / would bother to publish / Alfred Martinez or go hear / him read? But A. Ginsberg, / that's another matter." Alfred takes his pseudonym so seriously that when his father moves in with him, he too adopts the surname Ginsberg, to avoid confusion. This effort, however, is short lived when the father begins to write poetry as well and, since his name is Alfredo, takes the professional name A. Ginsberg.

Though the speaker, Antonio, also a struggling poet, gravitates toward Alfred to learn how to be successful in placing poems in literary magazines, and to poke through Alfred's bookshelves, "adding to [his] literary education," it's also clear that what keeps him coming back is this loving father-son relationship. Mr. Martinez is supportive of his son's creativity, choosing to stop writing poetry so that his son can claim the entire spotlight. Mr. Martinez explains, "I had a career. Forty years / with the post office delivering / mail, snow and rain. It's / his chance now to get ahead." Antonio's experience is markedly different:

> "I wish I had had a dad like you.
> I wish I had had a dad period
> even if he had been mean and beat me
> as long as he had taken me
> to some ball games and fishing."
> "That's right, you didn't know
> your dad," says Mr. Ginsberg.
> "That's right," I say. "My mom
> had me to increase the welfare check."

A dramatic turn of fates takes place when, for some unexplained reason, Alfred throws his father out of the house. Alfred's career begins to flourish while Antonio is stuck in anonymity, unpublished and unrecognized. When Alfred arranges a poetry reading for his friend, no one shows up, not even Alfred himself. Dejected, Antonio returns yet again to his incomplete opus, a 1,000-page poem, of which he has written only 160 pages. "Only 840 to go," he says.

Meanwhile, Alfred's phone rings constantly, so he decides to purchase an answering machine. It captures Mr. Martinez's pleading voice to be allowed back in, along with the voices of the dead Beat writers who have "been calling him for months. / They've become abusive / calling him at all hours / of the day and night / accusing him of plagiarizing." The disruption of harmony between Alfred and Mr. Martinez takes place once Alfred transforms into A. Ginsberg entirely. Alfred has a father; A. Ginsberg no longer does. A. Ginsberg becomes so famous he even excels in a second artistic discipline, painting. Eventually, it is revealed that buried inside Alfred is another name, Francisco, demonstrating Alfred's commitment to distancing himself from his Mexican identity to assimilate and thrive in an Americanized one. Antonio, who is given the name Pablo (as in Neruda), sinks deeper into despair. When he finally takes his manuscript to Fulgenzi (a nod to Ferlinghetti in an Italianized version of the Mexican name Fulgencio), the editor shatters Antonio's confidence by telling him, "I think you should take it out / into the country and bury it / before it stinks up this town."

If making it in the poetry business means selling out, Antonio is hesitant to do so, but the punishment for adhering to his artistic integrity is a slow descent into obscurity. It's a state of anguish that he must climb his way out of each morning—a Sisyphean cycle that allows him to cope with his professional failure but also with his fractured childhood:

> *I wake up*
> *and find that*
> *I am still myself.*
> *I would like*
> *to wake up*
> *some morning*
> *as someone else.*
> *And not remember*
> *who I was before.*
> *And not remember*
> *that I changed.*
> *I would not be me.*
> *I would be anyone else.*
> . . . .
> *But if I gave it*
> *serious thought*
> *I'd realize*
> *there are plenty*
> *of people*

who I'd hate to be.
That I could be
much worse off
than I am.

It's difficult to summarize a principal lesson from *San Fernandez Beat* without resorting to platitudes, so suffice it to say that what begins as a portrait of an artist as a young man ends in a more nuanced conversation about the folly of fame and fortune in America.

Beyond Nageezi brings Romero full circle to the small places that generate big moments. Measuring just over fourteen square miles, Nageezi is in the northwest section of New Mexico, one of the famed corners of the Four Corners region. Its population in 2020 was just under three hundred, 99 percent identifying as Native American. Its name comes from the Navajo word for squash. Close to seven thousand feet above sea level, Nageezi sits in the expansive high desert that's celebrated for its breathtaking natural beauty: rivers, valleys, buttes, and mesas have existed here since "time immemorial," to borrow a phrase from the Native American writer Leslie Marmon Silko.

In Romero's newest collection of poems, however, the speaker's journey to this part of New Mexico is a means of reflection—an assessment of what has transpired thus far in his life: "When I reach Nageezi / I know I have grown / immeasurably old / And that I have driven / here too fast." He is no longer the young man in *During the Growing Season* and *Agua Negra*, who was seeking orientation during the early years of adulthood. He has reached a mature age, when the questions become existential, warranting peaceful solitude and meditation. Hence the opening salvo:

I have come a long way
lured by the silence
and desolation
of the desert
to hold counsel
with the cactus

The speaker adopts a melancholy tone, and as a seasoned writer, he's more attuned to his creative process, which includes wandering through the natural landscape that inspires him and prompts his memory cells. *"I have come after visions, / you will sing / After poems,"* he tells himself. But there's an important component to this journey: he has come to Nageezi to contemplate mortality. Amid the evidence of a thriving natural world, he finds more visceral signs of deterioration, death, and loss. When he picks up a sun-bleached bone, he thinks "of the heart / and brain long gone." He comes across a severed coyote leg, bits of rabbit fur, and dried yucca—all reminders of the critical cycle of life and death, which includes humanity. Much later in the book, on another road trip, his mind returns to the harsh facts of life when he drives past a cemetery:

> *I thought about the people*
> *buried there*
>
> *They had families,*
> *friends, jobs, homes*
> *So many things*
> *But in death all they have*
> *is the grave they're in*
> . . . .
>
> *I have nothing*
> *but memories*

Worth mentioning is that during his pensive moods, the speaker doesn't entertain the notion of an afterlife, whether it's Catholic or informed by any other doctrine. He does mention at one point, "In centuries past / men came to the desert / to converse with God," and that he recalls "the madmen of the Bible, / saints, wandering the deserts," though he doesn't see his quest as religious. He didn't come here to dialogue with a deity. He arrived to ponder his path and its imminent conclusion. For him, the end is simply the end, though that doesn't necessarily mean that life becomes meaningless with death. Those two lines, "I have nothing / but memories," are spoken with ambivalence. If "nothing" refers to the material possessions that the dead cannot take with them, as a living person the speaker is either alluding to his own material poverty or comparing the value of material wealth to the richness of lived experience. Indeed, all he has are memories, but they are what empowers his creativity. It's a sentiment similar to Toni Morrison's philosophical proclamation: "We die. That may be the meaning of life. But we do language. That may be the measure of our lives."

A second distinct feature in *Beyond Nageezi* comes to light in the poem "The Cactus Have Taken Steps." Here, Romero employs a technique that he seldom uses in his work: anthropomorphism.

> *The cactus have taken steps*
> *toward their destruction*
> *They have begun to communicate*
> *in convoluted language*
>
> *The sky has taken hold of its skin*
> *and ripped it off*
> *Pearls of blood are dripping*
> *onto the outstretched palms of the mountains*
>
> *The white rocks have grown wings*
> *and flown away like gulls*
> *Fish are flopping in the sands*
> *alerting the horizon with their screams*

This begs the question of whether these images are allegories and metaphors for human behavior. If so, this opens the door to more complex readings of other anthropomorphic moments in this collection, like the turtles that "march / suicidally across the highway" and the jackrabbits that "froze / like convicts / as the headlights / swept over them." The collusion (or collision) of the animal and human realms gesture toward a grim or fatalistic view of the world. But Romero is kind to the reader because he makes sure to include symbols of hope and perseverance:

> *It is spring*
> *and tiny plants*

> *are breaking*
> *asphalt and concrete*
>
> *I feel heartened*
> *seeing those conspirators*
> *at work*

Despite the title, the speaker doesn't spend the entire time in Nageezi, though it is an important point of departure into the past. Several other destinations are mentioned—Clovis, Santa Rosa, Taos, Los Alamos, to name a few—mostly attached to memories. But that's the power of Nageezi—it has facilitated time travel to the various locations that hold special significance for the speaker. He recalls his impoverished childhood, relationships with women that ended in heartbreak or heartache, but also women who awakened his passions— love, romance, and desire. And that fictitious character Celso makes a surprise appearance. He's the unshakable, unkillable eccentric who demands to be part of this conversation, even if he's not the center of attention. That journey to the bittersweet past is so exhausting that at one point the speaker quips, "What else is there to remember / There should be pleasanter memories."

Beyond Nageezi closes with the title poem. The speaker keeps asserting that "beyond Nageezi / there is nothing / no matter / what the map shows." This is not a pejorative statement made against that tiny New Mexico town, because at this point it's evident that the speaker is talking not in geographical terms but in metaphysical ones. Beyond Nageezi—where life still flourishes—is complete darkness, the final mystery, the great unknown. The speaker, closer to that beyond, finally arrives at this honest but heart-wrenching conclusion:

> *Now I have grown wiser*
> *but no happier*
> *knowing that all things come to an end*
>
> *And I am reminded*
> *of who we are*
> *Transient, shimmering light*
> *within a body*

Though these are not Romero's final poems (he's already busy shaping the next poetry collection), *Beyond Nageezi* brings a satisfying sense of completion to this cycle of six books, a sextet nearly five decades in the making that reflects his stages of life and his development as a poet. Indeed, we are fortunate to trace the growth of the artist through this record of his creative productivity. Romero's poems, written with much patience and sincerity, remind us that journeys well contemplated are journeys well lived.

After revisiting the compelling poems of Leo Romero, I'm disheartened that over the years his work has not received more critical or literary attention, which it merits. The aptly named selected and new volume, *Trees Dream of Water*, aims to address those oversights by bringing new readers to his poetry and renewed interest in his creative body of work. But above all, I am hopeful that the next generation of poets will connect with Romero, who is a literary elder and a formidable role model because he's still creating and wrestling with the crucial questions of his time. And ours.

—*Rigoberto González*

TREES DREAM OF WATER

During the Growing Season

Season

(1978)

I HEAR THE MARE NEIGH

Breaking earth all day
back bent
fingers stiff
Sun set an hour ago
but I can't stop
Occasionally I try
to stand straight
and gaze up and down
the valley
which is fading away
I hear the mare neigh
for the fiftieth time
Lizardo took the stallion
to the mountains
hours ago
I bend again
and hit the earth
with my dull hoe

My feet feel planted
my muscles are old roots
When the moon
rises over the trees
I stand straight
something is coming down
from the mountains in waves
I have smelled it before
warm and bitter
I hear a nervous neigh
from somewhere by the river

IF THERE WAS MOONLIGHT

The first year I planted
I had to water
the small patch of corn
with buckets of water
from the spring
which was downhill
a hundred yards or so away
I would start
a couple of hours before sunset
and if there was moonlight
I would stay out late
When the first rain fell
I stood with the corn
and watched the drops of water
roll down the broad leaves
That first rain
hardly wet the ground
But it wasn't long
before it started
raining every day
I would check the corn
in the morning and afternoon
to see how much it had grown
I would poke the muddy ground
with a stick
and always find some living thing
extending roots
I was afraid to disturb
the ground too much
there might be veins
bones, a heart
But weeds grew everywhere
and I spent hours
pulling them
Yet for all that work

the frost killed everything
By mid-August
all the corn plants were dead
For many days after
I would spend hours
among the dried corn
watching and thinking
how they were like stiff ghosts
And on certain cold nights
I would walk through them
if there was moonlight

NO STARS NO STARS

Last night frightened wings
kept me awake
Wings brushed against the walls and ceiling
Tiny tremoring wings

Claws scratched the door
Claws scratched the glass

No moon no moon
in the eyes of the creature
that circled about the house
The odor of deep woods in its breath

No stars no stars
The frightened wings
brushed against the fur of night
The round ball of darkness

YOU LISTEN TO THE CHICKENS

At a certain time
you can see the darkness
step from behind the trees
in the mountains

And very soon
it is at your doorstep
All you can do
is shut the door

And again you hear
that *other* breathing
Those measured footfalls
cautious as a prowling moon

You listen to the chickens
in their wire cages
This late at night
you listen to the chickens

NOT OF THE SOIL

When the women wash
their clothes at the river
they often sing

If we were the fish in the river
the men would come after us
with hooks and line
with hunger in their eyes

The women wash their clothes
among the rocks
and hang the clothes
on the bushes to dry

Returning home from the fields
the men always stop to look for fish
They are hungry for something
not of the soil

RED DRESS

A little bird
flew over the mountain
to sing to me
A little bird
of pure song
singing about the graces
of your heart
bounteous as a garden

A little bird sat
upon my shoulder
and sang about you
He said he saw
your red dress
fluttering in the wind
like a God-bird

That same red dress
I saw you wear
at your cousin's wedding dance
When you danced
like a ball of fire
My hands burned
when we danced together
I swear—they burned

A little bird has come
to sing to me
about your heart
bright as any sun
which you show
so casually
that all mistake it
for a dress

WAY OF THE FALLING RAIN

From their homes in the trees
the cicadas make their sounds
Coming from the throats of the rain,
from the dry tongues of the earth
A moving of feet and shaking rattles
Necklaces of corn and turquoise swaying
This is the way of the falling rain

Overhead clouds are becoming mountains
The rain is silent as the deer
The rain is running like frightened deer
The cicadas have changed into men
Waving green branches and beating the ground
Men without voices and copper bells
This is the way of the falling rain

CHACÓN AND RAIN

It was raining lightly at Chacón
I would look at the mountains
and small rain clouds were rising
appearing like smoke signals
Or forest fires just beginning
There was much to do at Chacón,
at my grandmother's house,
which had not been lived in for a while
My leg went through the rotting floor
And the house was full of scuttling bugs
with spiders everywhere
The house where I was born
Where my grandfather was dying
of prostate cancer, and I was told
to sit in the room with him
At age ten sitting against the wall
not knowing what to do
People coming and going,
and I don't know that I said
anything to my grandfather
He only knew Spanish,
and I didn't feel comfortable
speaking in Spanish
though it was my first language
until I was about four
I sat there, the time passing slowly
when there were no visitors
Then suddenly someone would enter
the room, tearful or somber
No one seeming to notice me
I sat there not fully understanding
that my grandfather was dying
He didn't acknowledge my presence
and seemed to have to draw deep
from within himself for the energy
to meet yet another visitor
Attempting each time a weak smile

COMANCHITO LULLABY

1.
Dance to the Comanchito
The moon is in its fullness

Abuelita, Wake Me!
I am having that dream again

Dance to the Comanchito
To the music of centuries

I was looking for those balls
that grow on the oak leaves
that pop when you smash them

Listen to the music
It will connect with your blood

I didn't mean to go so far

The night is never ending
Come and dance with me

The sunflowers were without motion

When the moon is fallen
yet dance to the Comanchito

The Indians are coming
through the trees
Leaves falling like in autumn
The red and orange leaves of autumn

Dance to the Comanchito
The rhythm is in your blood

The Indians are angry with me
Abuelita, wake me!

2.
Wake up my grandson!
Why do you fear the Indians?
Do you remember
your grandfather's face?

It was not a Spaniard's face
Many who saw your mother
for the first time
called her Indita

I'd laugh when she'd say,
"I'm not a little Indian"

"Piensan que eres,
they think you are," I'd say
You look like me, hijito,
what can you do?
It's what we are

Do not fear what is
in your blood, my grandson

Go to sleep now
The swallow sleeps
The butterfly sleeps
Soon you too will sleep

WHAT TREES DREAM ABOUT

Trees dream of water
They dream of oceans full of water
They wake up children
in the middle of the night
and make them thirsty

In their dreams
trees uproot themselves
They flee from people
and become fish

Fishermen come after them
with enormous nets
Just as the trees wake up

PAST PLACITAS

Past Placitas
we pull off
to the side of the road
and spend hours
searching through hills
and arroyos

What are we looking for?
We'll know when we find it

As it grows late
we leave our search
After taking one last look
at the eroding hills
The wind-twisted piñon
and juniper
The red and yellow
escarpments

As we drive back
to Albuquerque
I think of what we found

A cactus growing out
of a dead one
Small, stiff brownish ferns
growing in rock crevices

And a metal crucifix
below an incline of the road
Brother Juan Rodriguez
1904–1922

THERE'S THE HOUSE

There's the house
Gray cement like it was
years back when Joe lived
there, it doesn't look
any worse
It was a dump then
Except the windows
are now boarded up
In the summer evenings
Joe's mother would sometimes
stand outside her door
A skinny, nervous woman
watching out for bats
that would try to steal
her lit cigarette
Joe and I would dig tunnels
through the weeds
and we'd hear
drunken laughter
coming from Joe's house
One day I heard Joe
and Antonio and Manny
in the wooden shack
next to Joe's house
and they were talking
about me
and laughing
I walked away upset
They never knew
I heard them

WE SLEPT ON THE PORCH

We slept on the porch
all summer
and we could hear them
flying over us
like a nearby river

They came so close
that sometimes
they brushed against
our sleep

We asked our neighbors
about them
but they sleep indoors
with the windows shut

"Your house is as full
of dreams
as mine is
as full of flies,"
an old man said
jealously

"Hush," his grandson said
"It is bad enough
that we don't dream
Don't wish it on others"

"Here," the old man said
pointing to a pile
of smooth rocks
higher than his house

"That is our shame,"
the young man chided
"Let them be"

We went home
thinking of what
their dreams
had become

And still did not know
what it was
that passed
at night
toward some
unnamed sea

THE ROAD TO WALDO

The road to Waldo
is full of cows
You'll find them
at all hours
Even in the middle
of the night
A disoriented look
in their eyes
as if brought there
by a flying saucer
from a planet
where there are
too many cows

When you see
that disoriented
look in their eyes
you know you are
in Waldo
That and a sign
along the railroad
tracks
are all that give
it away

Waldo is a state
of mind
cows sometimes
find themselves in
contemplating
their futures
as hamburgers
is what
I've concluded

AS CELSO TELLS IT

As Celso tells it
he shot at three coyotes once
and hit one
The one he shot fell
but the other two
helped him up
and all three
made it over the hill
Celso was so surprised
that he didn't dare
take another shot

One night some friends
were visiting Celso
In the middle of saying something
he began crying
like a coyote
His friends stared at him surprised
When Celso finally stopped
they asked him to do it again
"No," Celso said,
"they're gone, they're gone"

MENTIRAS

Celso is a good liar
He said he heard a sad angel
crying in the mountains

When Porfirio was grieving
the death of his wife
Celso claimed he saw
four ships take her away

What about when he told everyone
of the mute who sang
And the deaf man who listened
Of the blind man who saw
death get away

YAQUI INDIAN BLOOD

Erlinda, you with your Yaqui
Indian blood
and then some
some some other

Erlinda have I told you that
being with you
is warmth

You with your Yaqui blood
and I hate to make tortillas
attitude

HER NAME IS MORNING

Her name is morning
Her face is horizon
She has long hair
that touches the branches
She is no one's woman
and she cares for no one
Not even sun
who is so strong

Crow chides her
"Be a man's woman"
She is strong
and her legs are trees
And when she moves
the crows fly away crying
Her name is morning
She belongs to no one

LETTER TO ERLINDA

Left Albuquerque heading east
Spent the night in a building at
a rest stop near the Texas border
The building was rocking all night
There was a tornado that
struck Lubbock, I headed back
for Albuquerque the next morning
Got a ride through Albuquerque
and heading north, Denver, got
dropped off in Wyoming near
the Nebraska border, Got a ride
to Alliance before it got dark, Spent
the night in an all-night laundromat
sleeping on a wooden bench
A woman woke me up screaming in
my face not to steal her children's
clothes, That she had to go to church
I muttered I wasn't interested
in her children's clothes, fell
back asleep, when I woke up
she was folding clothes at a table
Seeing me awake she came
over to me and gave me a paper
bag with a processed-cheese sandwich,
a small bag of potato chips, an apple
I ate the sandwich and chips while
she watched me, I saved the apple
for later on the road, she asked
where I was going, I didn't really
know, just hitchhiking, seeming
to be heading east (In the back of
my mind I was thinking of coastal
Maine, a crazy idea), You have a map?
she asked, I did and she spread
it on the floor and we got on the floor

together, she traced a route with
her finger suggesting I could go
that way, east, and she told me that
she was a widow with two young
children, and if I went that way
she said I would go past her farm
She had to go somewhere but
if I went hitchhiking out by a
small bridge she told me about,
and if I was there when she
came by, she could show me
her farm, I hitchhiked by that
bridge for a couple hours, people
passing by there going to isolated
farms, staring at me as if I were
a Martian or something worse
Then I walked to the other side of
town and hitchhiked heading south
on a road with more traffic, even so
it took me all day to reach the eastern
outskirts of Bridgeport and there
I decided to head east and just got
a ride before the sun set, and now
I'm in Omaha soon heading for
Des Moines, Iowa, with a man who
claims to be a songwriter but seems
like a con man but he can't con me
out of anything, I don't have anything
but a few dollars, Oh, I ate the apple
last night, my only food in two days

HITCHHIKING

1.
Hitchhiking across
the spreading out
land of farmlands

My God! A sightless sun

No tomorrow or yesterday
Only a too-real today
through small towns
in a tornado's wind

Across mountains and plains
I die too much for this land

People's stares
Afraid
Too involved in their security
In their Cadillacs, Plymouths
to chance giving
a hitchhiker a ride

Sleeping on a wooden bench
in an all-night laundromat
in Alliance, Nebraska

Spending a night
at a rest stop
near the Texas border
while a tornado hits Lubbock

In a car
crossing Indiana and
Ohio at night

My life is good
but so hard to live

2.
I hitchhike
in this great land
with America screaming
in my ears
With its nose turned up at me
With me
alone
My body bursting with life

Rushing into America
with my arms wide open

GREEN SOMETHING OR OTHER

IN KANSAS

Dropped off in Kansas City, Missouri,
in the middle of the night,
off to the side of the freeway
Seeing skyscrapers
The furious late-night traffic
of a large city, the couple
I had gotten a ride with
in Iowa near Missouri
were screaming at me
to get out, I had fallen asleep
and they hadn't bargained
on giving me such a long ride
They sped off and I was
wondering what to do
Not possible to hitchhike
so late at night along the
screaming traffic, I climbed
up a small incline and tried
to sleep on the grass,
wrapping myself
in a thin plastic sheet
Soon woke up shivering in
the cold, the dew, walked
along the freeway until I got
to the toll bridge crossing the
Missouri River to Kansas
City, Kansas
At the tollgate I was told
I couldn't walk across, The bridge
was only for vehicles, I walked
back and then down an on-ramp
thinking it was better to hitchhike
where the traffic was

entering the freeway
I was expecting not to get a ride
that late at night but got lucky
A semitruck stopped and the man
said I could sleep in his berth
It took me a while to fall asleep
The water sloshing around
in my otherwise empty stomach
kept me awake
When I woke up
the trucker had pulled off
to the side of the road, end
of the road for me, almost
the entire length of Kansas
crossed while I slept
At the outskirts of a small town
called Green something
or other
Saw a restaurant with
a sign in the window
advertising their breakfast special
Still had some money left
from the ten dollars I had
started with almost
a week before
Ordered the breakfast special,
ate it slowly savoring
every bite
Thought of Erlinda
in Albuquerque
Thought of writing ·
her a letter
(probably didn't)
Thought of how I was getting
closer to New Mexico
Could be there by that night if lucky

IF WE GOT MARRIED

If we got married
How could we live?
I have no money
No car

That time I went to see you
unannounced
I rode my bicycle
more than twelve miles

Your father answered the door
and coldly said
you weren't there

So I made my way
back home
You happened to go by me
in a car with your sisters
you told me later

You said they laughed
not knowing who I was
A crazy guy on a bicycle
in heavy traffic

No doubt that made you
wonder about me
So many things have made
you wonder about me

You want to have
ten children you told me
But how can I support you
and children?

When I'm barely getting by
going to college
And no car
That's always an issue

Agua Negra

(1981)

IN THE RINCÓN

My grandmother would tell me
of the cold
sweet spring water
in the Rincón
She would go there
when she was newly married
And once she saw a bear
who had come down
from the mountains
for chokecherries
She fled and never returned
to the Rincón
a portion of land
far from any house
My grandmother is over eighty
She has forgotten much
But she has never forgotten
how cold and sweet
the water is in the Rincón

BENEDICTION

My grandfather and I
rode on a large workhorse
to the Rincón
a section of farming land
below the mountains
He stopped along the way
and took a piss
That is the earliest memory
I have of him
A few years later
he lay in bed
dying from cancer
I would sit quietly
in his room
on a chair against the wall
His hair was as white as God's
and people would come
to ask for his forgiveness

TREES

My grandfather is buried
by these three tall pines
in the Romero graveyard

He planted those plum trees
which gave bitter fruit
and no one liked to eat
until the trees died from neglect

He also planted these
stunted apple trees
which make a great show
of white blossoms
but the apples are small and few

The fruit trees
were my grandmother's idea
My grandfather complained
that it was too high and cold
for fruit trees
But my grandmother's thoughts
were with the orchards
of her childhood

The locusts and lilac bushes
were also my grandmother's idea
She kept her memories
and perplexed my grandfather

And those twenty-foot willows
where the magpies build their nests
were also planted by my grandfather
for my grandmother's sake

But my grandmother
didn't have anything to do
with planting those three pines
She was a Sanchez
Only the Romeros would think
of planting pines

THE GOAT'S CRY

My grandmother took the young goat
and slit its throat
Delicate cords cut in the glass air
I fled from the sharp knife
from the gush of hot blood
which had stained my grandmother's hands
which the earth drank greedily
In the air the goat's cry
shattered clouds
Opened and closed blue doors
I cowered inside the house
where I ran after seeing the sun's face
in the blade of the knife
Saw the sun drinking the blood

I listened to the incessant crying
The goat's agony
filling the sky like smoke
I was helpless and trembling
listening to the severed throat
To the blood cry
Elastic cords snapping
A cry jagged as broken glass
until the goat's cry finally left the sky
and my grandmother was calling me
to wash my hands
to drink of the blood
The still hot blood
which she held in a pan
A pool of life
Bright life

ESTAFIATE

My grandmother walked slowly
on thin legs
Her body bent forward
by her humped back
which she had gained
with the years
and made her look
as if she were sinking
into the earth
or shrinking back
into a child

She walked fragilely
on slippered feet
and seldom left the house
except to pick estafiate

She'd boil it
into a greenish tea

She would tell me in Spanish
the names of herbs
she had picked
when she was younger
But now all
that she could find
was estafiate

Each day she seemed
to grow weaker
It was summer
but she would sit
by the woodstove
dressed in housecoat and slippers
Keeping the fire burning
saying that she felt cold

And she was always
boiling some estafiate
which she claimed
was the "best medicine"

TOO MANY YEARS

"Once there were too many people
in the valley,"
my grandmother told me
And she shook her head
from side to side

"But most of the people
have died
or moved away"

My grandmother closed
her eyelids
And opened them slowly

Yes, it was true, many houses
were falling into ruin
The fields hadn't been planted
in years

"The houses were too pretty,"
she continued,
"With Castilian roses
and hollyhocks

And the fields were
too pretty
Full of all kinds of food"

Her old dim eyes
looked toward the cattails

"There I grew rhubarb for pies
and medicine"

My grandmother seemed pleased
saying that,
sitting on her porch
from which she had
a sweeping view of the valley,
el Valle de San Antonio

"When did people first come
to this valley?" I asked

My grandmother was astonished
by my question
She gave me a thoughtful
look
Then looked out
over the valley at nothing
in particular

"Too long for anyone to remember,"
she finally said in Spanish
"Maybe Don Antonio knew
but he's been dead
too many years"

AGUA NEGRA

Outside, the night lay open
like an oyster
I sat alone
within my house
of light

Within the mountains
darkness poured like syrup,
poured into that black
which filled the valley
like the deepest ocean

I would hear the throbbing
of the mountains
The slow breathing of trees
and sense the uneasiness
of the fields

I thought of the miracle
at Agua Negra
where people searched
with tiny lights
for the face of God

A SHADOW WHICH COULD BE

ANYTHING

Cecilia drew a picture of the miracle
at Agua Negra, a shadowy shape
slightly reminiscent of the Christ depicted
on calendars, a shape in the newly
plastered wall of an old house
next to the church, Rumor was
that nuns had once taught school there

Cecilia had the drawing reproduced
and each night she would sit at a small
folding table offering her drawing for sale
to the hundreds who would come
to see how the streetlight would cast
a miraculous vision against an ordinary wall

Cecilia was not ashamed nor embarrassed
when asked how she could be so sacrilegious
"It was the Luceros who started it all,"
she'd say, "selling tamales to the multitudes
They have a large house with two new rooms
I have but my one-room adobe house
with woodstove and bed side by side
No running water and a drafty outhouse
Why shouldn't I make a little profit
from a miracle, otherwise what good is it?"

For nights Cecilia tried to sell her drawings
yet she barely broke even, Otero
from the Gambels' store in Vegas
had done a painting wild in its use
of imagination, He had summarized the Bible
and placed it all on the plain wall
in which everyone saw such wonders

and his reproduced painting sold
by the hundreds making him rich
Or at least he was able to buy a new truck

Cecilia could not understand it
She had painted the truth, dull
and ordinary as it might be, nevertheless
hardly anyone recognized it

"The miracle at Agua Negra,"
people would say, "it can't be
We've seen it, demons and angels,
the Virgin and the Christ, everything
we have been taught to believe is there
like in Otero's painting, He has captured it
But your drawing, what does it show?
A dark shadow which could be anything"

THE SILENT BELL

In the church in Santa Gertrudes
there is a bell made out of silver and gold
But there is a flaw and it has never sounded
It is over a hundred years old
People come from far away to see this bell
The priest says that it is
like the great bell in heaven
which rings constantly and yet goes unheard
If we could hear such a lovely sound we'd die
Our souls, the priest says, are drawn
to this silent bell
because the heavenly bell is made of gold and silver
And the sound is so pure that not even dogs
can hear it

THE TREES ON THE HILLSIDE

The trees on the hillside
form a distinctive silhouette
against the twilight sky
Caught between day and night
they mesh together
forming a wall, a boundary

The trees on the hillside
have become a part
of the geography of my mind
A means of marking out
my existence
when maps fail to tell us
where we are at

AUGUSTINA

The day Porfirio's wife died
he carried her to the wagon
and covered her with a quilt
she had made
when they were first married

A young boy herding goats
saw Porfirio driving the wagon
over the rocky ground
then disappear into the mountains
There was something in the wagon
But when Porfirio returned later
the wagon was empty
The young boy herding goats
whistled, but Porfirio did not look at him
The goats fled from Porfirio
and the young boy followed them

On his way home
Porfirio paused at Contrario's house
He did not get off the wagon
"My wife is dead," Porfirio said
and he told the horse to get moving
Word spread quickly
that Porfirio's wife had died
Many people came to his house
and brought food
No one lingering
He wasn't one for conversation
Her name was Augustina
She was the last Indian
to live in the valley

WEAVING THE RAIN

I smell the first rain of this spring
and leave the door open
I am reminded of a feeling I had yesterday
while looking at a map of New Mexico
I was overcome by a sense of enormous space
and I caught a whiff of a wind
carrying rain, and I felt the grama grass
moving around me, spreading for hundreds
of miles

Outside, the wind is weaving the branches
with their sprays of young leaves
and flowers
The wind deftly weaving the rain
into darkness
as the trees wave

A LYING MOON AND A LONELY BIRD

I search for a history of this valley
but no one wrote it down
so I look for anything
For a scrap of paper
with a few words
but I find nothing other
than some names and dates
written in family bibles
I am left to construct a history
where there are no written records

I wander through the mountains
hearing faint noises
but never seeing anything
I spend hours planting
and in my dreams I see
old-fashioned writing
which turns into roots
I wake up nights and hear
someone leafing through a book
I turn on the light and there is nothing
I hear footsteps outside
I hear the moon spinning tales
I turn off the light and lay awake

Far away a bird is calling
when it should be asleep
and I want to call back
I want to speak so all of the night
and silence can understand me
like this bird, but the moon
continues his tales undisturbed
I listen, perhaps I will write it down
and say, This is how the people
lived in the valley, a lying moon
and a lonely bird say it all

THIS DARK WINTER

This dark winter night
I think of my mother
as I drive
through dark hills
past small villages
that flicker for a moment
and then are lost

Beyond these hills
are mountains
I cannot see
But I feel them,
their oceanic presence
I carry them
within me, always
Massive rock mountains

Often as a child
I would see you look
out the window
The fatalism of mountains
in your eyes
A certain heaviness
of rocks and pine

I think back
to what you said
as I left
and your eyes were
on the overcast mountains
That it might snow

Perhaps even now
the pure-white crystals
are taking shape·

And I think back
to the heaviness
of mountains
in your eyes

How soon these mountains
will descend
like the snow
I am now catching
glimpses of
in the headlights

LEAVING VEGAS

I feel harassed by the wind
Not until I reach the mountains
does it lessen

I drive in the direction
of the high mountain valley
where I was born

I soon pass the turnoff to Chacón
and take a quick glance
out across the San Antonio Valley
where I haven't been in years

I climb Holman Hill,
actually a mountain,
heading for Taos

I think of my trip to Vegas
to see my mother
I couldn't wait to leave home
when I graduated from high school
ten years ago
and left for Albuquerque
in a matter of days

To the east of Vegas
the plains stretch out to Texas
To the west the Rocky Mountains

I couldn't have stayed in Vegas
any longer than I did
Not this time
nor ten years back

Nothing has changed
Especially the persistence
of the wind
I don't understand
why the town hasn't blown away

THERE IS THE WIND

There is the wind and mountains
And the heavy wings of the bird

There is a thin-walled house
newly painted
Inside, my aging mother sits
Her chair against the living room wall
She peers at her arthritic hands
with a vacant gaze and then
brings one hand toward her face

The bird's heavy wings cannot lift it
above the indifferent wind and mountains

The artifacts of a life surround her
The television is silent for a change
The radio is on in the kitchen
but not being listened to
The worn carpet
And plastic flowers
on the dining room table
seen from the depth of aging eyes

The endlessly extending mountain
outside her kitchen window
Nothing of word but monotonous
in its angular silence of dark green
Metamorphosing into deeper silence
Into the remoteness of blue distance

MY MOTHER LISTENS

My mother listens
to the house creak
To the refrigerator's
continual hum
And to the noisy toilet
after it's flushed

At first, after her last
child left home,
she paced
about the house
not knowing
what to do
with her hands

They were
like wild birds
trying to escape

Now her hands
are captive
on her lap

Patiently
she waits and listens

The house creaks
with the wind trying
to come in
or call her out

ONE DAY BEFORE CHRISTMAS

1.

One day before Christmas
a man came to our door
and handed me a paper bag

Was he supposed to be Santa Claus?
Maybe he wore
a Christmas hat
It might have been something
the Rotary Club or one
of those civic groups
did before Christmas

I was around six
and still remember
the orange,
the apple,
the peanuts
And some hard
Christmas candy

2.

My mother and I stood
in line at a warehouse
to get food
the government gave
to the poor

The food was in bags
and cans that looked
like military rations
They all had the same
drab look with printing
on them that they
were government
commodities

Among the food items
such as rice, sugar,
dried milk was
a large can of
peanut butter
that was difficult to swallow

It would stick
to my upper mouth,
but mixing it with
a little pancake syrup
(also a commodity)
made it easier to swallow
and less bland

Sometimes my mother
made a little candy,
something we otherwise
seldom ate,
by melting some sugar
in a frying pan with lard

When the melted sugar
hardened, it was like
peanut-brittle candy
without the peanuts

As a result of eating
this pure-sugar candy,
my mother and I both
lost a molar
when we
developed a tooth infection
around the same time
and the tooth
had to be pulled out

After the middle
of the month,
when the money
from the welfare check
was nearly gone,
and the commodities
were disappearing fast,
we would get
reacquainted
with what it was like
to starve

It was something
that wore away at us
This continual
returning back
to having nothing

3.
My siblings were
7 to 10 years older than me
I hardly remember them
ever being around

Recently my sister
told me
about her
and my two brothers
going to visit
my aunt Mary
and my uncle Moises
and that aunt Mary
would feed them

I long suspected
they got meals
at friends' houses
or somewhere

BEFORE WE HAD AN ICEBOX

Before we had an icebox,
we would put a few
food items that needed
to be cold
on the window ledge

That must have been
before it got too cold
and before the summer

The tree outside our window
was an elm tree
I remember being
so hungry that I would
eat its leaves
until one day
I saw a green caterpillar
doing the same thing
and that revolted me

After we got an icebox,
I would take my toy wagon
across the river
to the icehouse
and get a block of ice
to put in our small icebox
that only contained a few things
like the opened can
of evaporated milk
that my mother
liked to put in her coffee

There was no electricity
Just the block of ice
until it melted
and I went out
with my wagon
for another block of ice
if we had the money

The toy wagon had been
an extravagant
Christmas present,
something I wouldn't have
ever dreamt of getting

I realize now
that my mother
got it on credit
(she got almost
everything on credit)
And strained to
pay for it
So we could get
commodities
And ice for the icebox

ARTIFICIAL FLOWERS

1.
Ahead
headlights coming
in my direction
then swishing by
Seldom seeing any lights
of houses
When they're seen
they're solitary lights
off at a distance
Or a tiny cluster
of lights
that are passed quickly

Then back
to the long miles
of darkness
with just the headlights
illuminating
the asphalt road
Not seeing far
ahead
Driving straight
into that darkness
that folds behind me
with the same heavy
darkness
as when I approached it

2.

I think of my mother when
she was young
and think of how
beautiful
and strong
she was
I think of her
now old
and think how
she's still beautiful
and how there
are still signs
of that strength

Everything dwindles in time
She was a tree
and grew to give full shade
Birds came
without knowing her
They lived within
and about her
and sang
And still they did not know her

I think of all this
as I see her
in the hospital bed
She doesn't have
the energy
to recognize me
And perhaps neither
the desire

3.

Coming back there are always
long miles to travel
Sixty miles seem
like four hundred
I arrive in daylight
and will be returning
at night
Even before I've arrived
I feel myself leaving
Already
my thoughts
are taking me away

4.

When she was a young
teenager my mother lived
in a mining town
where there are now
no traces of houses
She told me once
of a time
she was so ill
she thought she was
going to die
Her mother made her a soup
with garlic
And pressed ice
to the side of her stomach

I wonder
if she feels as sick
now
as she felt then
An old woman convalescing
from surgery
Suddenly I'm seeing
how old she is
Wasn't it just
a short while ago
that she was vigorous
and strong?

5.
I see myself lying
in that hospital bed
someday
A room shared
with a stranger
who has the TV
on all night
and even into the early
morning hours
I think of the crazed man
whose yells come
periodically
from down the hall
A patient
from the state
mental hospital
And I wonder
Will people come
or not come?
Will they gather
or not gather
around me
when I'm in my
hospital bed
old and sick?
And will it matter?

6.
When my mother
was twelve
her father went
to work at the mines
in Terreros

When she was thirteen
her father took
his family
with him

She immediately
went to work
cleaning
tourist cabins
nearby

Besides helping
the cook,
it was her responsibility
to strike the small
drum
announcing
the food was ready

It had only been
during
the last few years
that my mother
had told me
about the drum

It was a joyful
memory, a prideful
memory, how she stood
outside the door
standing straight
And beat the drum
for everyone to hear

And everyone came
because
of the drumming sound
she made

7.
After surgery
during short moments
of consciousness
my mother remembers
the artificial flowers
on her table at home

"Don't let anyone
take the flowers,"
she tells me
while still a bit dazed
Remembering when
her brother Moises
died
When relatives took
what they could

"Don't let anyone
take the flowers,"
she repeats
several times
She's remembering
the flowers
on her living room table

I remember her pointing
to them one day
and saying how beautiful
they were
I remember just glancing
at them and thinking
But they're
artificial flowers

8.
One part of dying
is like leaving Vegas
at night
I find myself thinking

That's because
by the time
I look
in the rearview mirror
I'm already down a hill
And there's no sign
of Vegas
except for
a faint glow
in the night sky
There's still
a faint light
in the sky
in the direction
I'm heading
Where the sun set

And I find myself thinking
This is like the first part
of dying
because the evening star
is visible
And soon there will be
enough stars
to make out constellations
Because this is
the first part of dying
And the real darkness
is yet to come

Celso

(1980) (1985)

CELSO WAS BORN

Celso was born right before Christmas
His father took one look at him
and left for good
muttering that his sins had come
to haunt him

Celso's mother died
shortly afterward
Some said it was from complications
from childbirth
Others said it was from grief
at losing her husband
Nevertheless there seemed
to be a smile on her face
as if she were relieved
to have escaped the burden
of bringing up Celso

Celso was brought up by his
spinster aunt who had long
prayed for a child
and thought of Celso as
God's answer to her prayers

Blessed was María
among all women
She was never married
And yet she had Celso as a son

CELSO'S FATHER

When he was a child
Celso was always being asked
who his father was

He died in the war
Celso would answer curtly

The war, people would say
Which war

The one in which he died
Celso would respond
and then turn about abruptly
and flee from their next question

People never let up
They hounded him about the matter
The only solution was to run

When other children
asked him who his father was
he found it easier
to continue the lie

His father had died in the war
It had been the last war
His father had been blown up
So there wasn't a grave

Celso avoided adults
like the plague

He never went into
his friends' houses
Their parents' first question
never varied

But when Celso became a man
and people would ask him
who his father was
He would answer them bluntly
that he was the product
of an immaculate conception
just like Jesus
but that he had no great plans
for the salvation of mankind ·

And damn if he'd die
on a cross
for their sins

THE MOON AND ANGELS

I remember once as a child
traveling at night
and watching the moon
It is following me, I thought
It is my own guardian angel
like the one pictured
in the catechism books

All holy things glow
The stars, the sun
The moon and angels
Celso, I thought to myself,
you are someone special
What have you done to make
the moon follow you like a dog

And I remembered that
I had been to confession that day
And when I walked out of the church
the world was different
Clearer, a little like heaven

When I had walked into the church
my heart had felt
like a dirty, ragged bag
filled with drowned kittens
But when I walked out the door
my heart was buoyant
Afloat in the air
Higher than any bird

That must be it, Celso,
I thought
The moon is attracted
to the pure silver
of your heart
untarnished by sin

And I reasoned that the moon
was the halo of an angel
looking down from heaven
And thus could be seen
the top of his head

ASH WEDNESDAY

Celso knelt before the altar
The priest pushed a thumb
against Celso's forehead

Everyone in Agua Negra
had an ashen thumbprint
on their foreheads

It was Ash Wednesday
and Celso staggered
out of the church

"Dirt, we are all dirt,"
Celso muttered
and scooped a palm full of dirt

He flung it in the air
And stared bleary eyed
at the enormous mountains

Celso turned his back
on the church
and walked aimlessly

HOLY WATER

For Easter, Celso put a sign
by the river reading
HOLY WATER—50 CENTS A BUCKETFUL
People were suspicious at first
How can you make such a claim
they would say
eyeing the river doubtfully

I had the priest bless the river
Celso would say
And now and forever
the flowing water of this river
will be holy water
But only between these two stakes
And Celso would point to two sticks
twenty yards apart

That is only as far
as the priest walked
before he fell into the river
and drowned thus becoming a saint
It is only while the water
is between these two stakes
that it is holy

THE MIRACLE

Celso had a vision
He saw the face of Jesus
on the wall of a small house
by the church in Agua Negra
He would pass there each night
on his way home from the bar
usually so drunk on wine
that he would see two of everything
And in fact he saw two Jesuses
though he knew there was but one

By next day everyone had heard
of Celso's vision
That night there were hundreds of people
from the many mountain villages
gathered to see the miracle
Some said they saw the face of Jesus
Others saw Satan, Mary, a lamb,
a cross, and someone even
claimed to see the Last Supper
Those who saw nothing were quiet

A THOUSAND ANGELS

Did you hear of when Celso
saw a thousand angels
dancing in the eye of a needle
He was sewing a button
when he suddenly heard music
and there they were, a thousand
angels dancing to a wild polka

It lifted me off my feet, said Celso
And I danced too
And those angels liked
my dancing so much
they made me promise
to dance with them again
when I go to heaven

ANGEL HAIR

Celso keeps three long strands
of white angel hair
in a metal box
When he gets drunk
he shows it to people
But tells them not to touch
or they will burn their hands

Where did you find this hair
people ask him
I woke up one night he says
and caught my guardian angel napping
I pulled his hair to teach him
to be more vigilant
And that is how I came to have
this withered hand

Not really a withered hand
But when he's drinking
Celso imagines all sorts
of defects

ESTRELLITA'S LIPS

Celso kissed Estrellita's lips
and they reminded him of wine
I get drunk every time I kiss her,
Celso would explain
to anyone who would ask if he was in love

Like cheap wine her lips
don't cost much
but they go straight to the head

The heart, the heart,
people would say
That is what matters, not the head

But Celso was adamant
The head is the house of the soul
The heart is a flea-bitten bed
A restless night, a terrible complaint
Only the head, the head
Adding, subtracting,
multiplying, such is love

UNA CANCIÓN DE FLORES

Listen to Celso
and you'd think anything was possible

Celso claims the moon is a woman
who carries a large knife
He has seen her cut down stars
which came too close

    Anoche la luna
    salió de los árboles
    con un cuchillo largo

    La luna tiene cabello blanco
    Ojos blancos
    Labios blancos

Celso has heard the moon sing
songs of flowers

Celso carries a long knife
to be like the moon
He tells everyone that he is in love
and brandishes the knife gently
as if he were beheading roses

TRISTE, TRISTE SON

Triste, triste son
los ojos
de los muertos
So sad are the eyes
of the newly dead
Who are they
looking at
Where does
their gaze wander
So sad are these eyes
that refuse to close
What could they see
Nothing, nothing
They see nothing
Triste, triste
son los ojos
de los muertos

THE DEAD ARE DANCING

The dead are dancing
under the full moon
They pretend to be drunk
They pretend to belch
and fart but no sounds
are heard only the clacking
of their bones

Unable to sleep because
of the clacking of bones
Celso looks out his window
and sees two skeletons
trying to kiss and make love
but they are frustrated
because they are nothing
but bones, and in frustration
they clack their bones
even louder

Stop making such a racket!
Celso screams out his window
But the skeletons only make
louder clacking sounds
Lost in their pretended
drunken merriment

You dead should have
the courtesy
of remaining dead
once you are buried!
Celso screams before
slamming his window shut
His head agonizing
from drinking too much

A DYING FLOWER FOR HIS HEART

Celso was watering his flowers
when a skeleton
who was passing by
stopped and asked
if he could have a flower

Thinking this skeleton could be
someone he once knew
Celso nodded yes

The skeleton picked a bright red flower
and placed it where
his heart had once been

I should have said, Any flower
but the red one, Celso thought
dismayed as he stared
at the skeleton walking away
with his favorite flower

The skeleton's bony fingers
holding the flower in place

THIS BITTERNESS

Celso, sit down and join me
in a glass of cheap wine
It's all I can afford these days

Celso, we were young together
and now we are old together
There is no escaping the years
They sweep over us like a wind
that wears us down

Celso, look at me honestly
and tell me
what it is that you see
I ask but I am afraid to know

Does it matter that I was born
and that I have lived this long
And all for what
Has it been a waste,
my life
Can a life such as mine
have mattered

No, please, don't answer, Celso
I just needed to get
that off my chest
What could you possibly say
And whatever you'd say
I'd probably be insulted

Here, let me pour you
a glass of my cheap wine
All I can afford these days
Let's forget what I said

Celso, you're grimacing
as you drink my wine
You are a true friend
Sharing this bitterness with me

THE SORROWFUL MADONNA

Celso has seen
the Sorrowful Madonna
in the form of Josefita,
a young widow
who lives in a cabin
a ways up the mountain

Celso has seen her
from a distance
emerging from the forest
and crossing fields of alfalfa
He still remembers her
as a young girl
riding her father's horse
to Agua Negra
for a few groceries

Celso's heart sings
like a psalm in the Bible
He is always picking
bouquets of wild flowers
which he will never give her

BECAUSE THE MOON IS A WOMAN

Because the moon is a woman
I love the moon, Celso says
to anyone who will listen

You see how far away the moon is
There is a reason

I loved Josefita so much that it hurt
But no matter how much pain
it caused me I went for more

And rather than see me suffer so much
she left me and became the moon

At nights I watch her
so cold and remote, I tremble a little
But the suffering is gone

People laugh at Celso

Josefita didn't become the moon
She's here, among us

An attractive young widow
who's hardly aware
Celso exists

JOB VISITS CELSO

One of the few times
that Celso
ever went to church
he heard a sermon
on Job

Now, he is a man
I can understand,
Celso thought

After that
Celso went around
telling everyone
that Job
had come to him
in a dream

What did Job
tell you,
people would ask
He complained
about the difficulties
of life, Celso sighed
And how unfair
God can be

What did you
say to that,
people would ask
on the verge of laughter
I offered him
some wine
And we got
good and drunk

Thinking for a minute
Celso continued

We traded complaints
about our lives
And before that night
was over
Job's old lips
actually cracked
a smile
And a few
thankful tears
flooded his eyes
at the thought
of someone
being worse off
than him

CELSO'S DREAM

Santiago, last night
I had a dream
in which the air
was filled
with skeletal angels

They swarmed
like millions of moths
obscuring the sun

And when they came
to earth
they sank
into the ground
into their graves

Leaving behind
only their wings
which rose
into the air

And it was then,
Santiago, that I heard
the heavenly
songbirds sing
this song

Farewell
to your earthly cages
The earth is welcome
to your bones
But heaven-bound
are your wings

CELSO TALKING TO THE MOON

I am afraid sometimes,
Celso says
as he licks the wine
off his lips

I am afraid of the blood
sweeping across my body

Celso takes a swig of wine

The problem is
that I fear life
as much as I fear death

Celso shivers even though
it is a warm night

You are lucky
You are a woman
Celso gazes longingly
at the moon

When you are afraid, you cry
Tears come easily to you

Celso takes a long drink
trying to get his heart so drunk
that it will let go
of a few miserable tears

ONE NIGHT AS CELSO

One night as Celso
stumbled home drunk
he noticed that the mountains
seemed to be dancing
But it was a slow
patient dance
done by black-veiled widows
A dance to make
the heart turn cold

He crossed his heart
and said, Blessed is the Virgin
And so is her child
So saying he felt
somewhat relieved

But he couldn't escape
the strange feeling
that the mountains
were in procession
to a funeral
Could it be my funeral,
he thought terrified
sobering up

After that Celso reduced
his drinking
unable to get that slow
patient dance out of
his head
That procession
of black-veiled widows
Not a dance
A funeral procession
to that hole in the ground
that awaited him

SANTIAGO, SINCE I TURNED SIXTY

Santiago, since I turned sixty
I am feeling anxious
about my old age

All my life I have lived
from day to day
And I have had the health
to live that way

But you see how much
white hair I have, Santiago
Old age is here

Everyone sooner or later
has to deal with
their old age, Celso says
A strain in his voice

But the other day you were talking
about wanting children,
Santiago says
Have you changed your mind

That was the wine talking
Celso says
Today I'm sober

THERE WAS A TIME

There was a time
it was a
pleasure to drink,
Celso says, but anymore
it has become a job

Celso dutifully empties
his glass of wine
and staggers to the door
of the bar

Thinking how he is
getting old
and has no children
Celso turns and says,
I have seen children
spit in their parents' eye

In the wind I can spit
in my own eye

But no one in the bar
is listening to him

Celso shuts the door
behind him
realizing he is done
with drinking

Going Home Away Indian

(1990)

GOING HOME AWAY

Going home away
Indian
is what he calls himself
And I got no horse
to ride, he says
And if I did
I wouldn't ride it
I would walk alongside it
as if it were my buddy
Funny-faced buddy
with big horse teeth
and big horse ass
I walk on home always
he says
and away
Secure in my green
cocoon blanket
And even if it were raining
fire
I'd walk on home
and away

HE WAS DANCING THE YELLOW DANCE

He was dancing the Yellow Dance
with six others
All of them wearing
some yellow
Not too many people
like to wear yellow anymore, he thought
as he danced
This is the way of going,
he thought
The yellow path of dancing
The sun's footsteps
We're dancing for
and with him, he thought
They danced all night
but to them it was like day
Dancing the Yellow Way

HE DIDN'T LIKE ME

He didn't like me
the first time
he saw me
He didn't see me
a second time
but I knew
he wouldn't have liked me
a second time
He was a Marine Indian
with his hair cut short
Why you hanging out
with this Mexican
I could see him thinking
as he talked with his brother
He seemed sore
at his brother
Maybe it was because his
brother wore long braids
like an old-time Indian
He was a new-time Indian
Sore as hell at everyone
Except his uniform
and the Marines
That saved him
from he's not sure what
Oh, yeah
Saved him from hanging out
with Mexicans
and wearing his hair long
like a traditional
Indian

IT WAS IN 1856

It was in 1856
he had his head
blown off
Direct hit
by a man
shooting
out of the train
at the buffalo
That was his worst
nightmare
He was dressed
in war regalia
A one-man war party
And before
he could put an arrow
in his bow
the man turned
from aiming
at a buffalo
and aimed
at him

IN HIS DREAMS

In his dreams
he rode naked
on a purple horse
Without a saddle
He held tight
to the mane
Naked wild Indian
in his dreams
with long braids
flailing
the prairie wind
But it's not
the prairie
he races across
but the ocean
A wide, endless
ocean
Leading his steed
westward
like the sun
A steed too wild
to tame
except in dreams
Racing
to awaken
the nations
out of their
deathly slumber
A dream awakening
a sleep
out of its
nightmare

SKELETON INDIAN

Skeleton Indian
He wears blue jeans
He wears a red
oxblood
colored shirt
He wears sunglasses
The women do come out
in the nighttime
They see him coming
Hey, Indian man
they say
We think you're cute
Skeleton Indian
grins at this
Cute, he says
Marilyn Monroe
is cute
Don't be offended
the women giggle
We see you're
manly
Big brave as you are
Still, cute is fine
for a man to be
And who's this
Marilyn
you're always
jabbering about
If we ever see her
we'll tear her dress off
and then some
Skeleton Indian
laughs out loud
Marilyn Monroe
is my skeleton Indian

She's not afraid
of any alive
plump women
like you
Many a woman
has tried
to scratch out
her eyes
but she hasn't got any
Skeleton Indian
won't mess around
with these barfly
women
when he's got
Marilyn Monroe Indian
at home

MARILYN MONROE INDIAN

It's all an illusion

Marilyn Monroe Indian
Luscious cactus
fruit lips
Tight sweater
and tight
black pants
She's got a movie star
look about her
Wind blows up
her dress
and everybody looks
Especially the women
What's she got
that we ain't got
they whisper among
each other
White man approves
of such shapely legs
You're going out
on the town
to Manhattan's
and Los Angeles's
fanciest
You couldn't do
any better
than with
Marilyn Monroe Indian
by your side
Beautiful as she is
she can even read
palms
And no one doubts
her acting abilities

anymore
Me, she says modestly
How could all this
fame
come to me
Little girl
who grew up barefoot
on the reservation
By way of explaining her
other Indians say
she belongs
to the long lost
tribe
of albino Indians
out by Zuni
or someplace

SKELETON INDIAN, HE'S THE TALK

Skeleton Indian
he's the talk
of the town
from hogan
to Pueblo
to tepee
to apartment complex
in Albuquerque's
SE Heights
Skeleton Indian
he's the talk
of the town
in his turquoise colored
boots
and Arrow shirts
This is no
government Indian
He's an escaped
Indian
No reservation
can hold him
for long
Indian girls
tell Skeleton Indian
Take us away
from the wide open
spaces
of reservation life
Girls in Indian schools
say
Take us away
from grades
and future days
as office workers
and computer operators

Take us away
they all ask him
Even urban Indians
make eyes at him
Take us to where
we haven't been
they're always
asking him
Skeleton Indian
just smiles
As much as a skeleton
can smile
that is
He doesn't mind
all of the attention
Being the talk
of the town
and all

I EVER SEE YOU

I ever see you
in this bar again
he says
I'll turn you
into a high
squeaky Mexican
A Mickey Mouse
of a Mexican
you hear
he says
This is an Indian bar
No Mexicans allowed
And if I ever see you
with an Indian woman
again
he says
I'll introduce
you to my friend
Skeleton Indian
He'll kick
your butt
into the grave
if I don't do it first
Scary Indian he is
He scares Indians
half to death
without meaning to
Mexicans
he don't like
His dad was killed
by a Mexican
outside a bar
in Gallup
He comes around
after 11 o'clock

Any Mexicans
around here
he'll say
What's your name again
Martinez or Rodriguez
What's that,
Raymundo
I'll remember
I won't forget
to introduce you
to Skeleton Indian
he won't like you
I can see
it's going
to be
a fun night after all

YELLOW BLOUSE WOMAN

Yellow Blouse Woman
I called her
She didn't appreciate that
Didn't even really have
an Indian name
until she named herself
Part Indian, part White
She had come to see herself
more and more
as an Indian
I didn't mean any harm
calling her Yellow Blouse Woman
It was almost the only blouse
I'd see her wear
Not quite
There must have been others
She wasn't that poor
And there was always Goodwill
and Salvation Army
But I swear that's all
I'd remember
That Yellow
in her smiles
and in her words
Like the sun rising
And I see it still
remembering her
after all these years

SKELETON INDIAN THINKS

Skeleton Indian
thinks
if anyone offered
to paint his portrait
it'd become
as famous
as the Mona Lisa
No lips
How does he smile
with no lips
people would ask
The painting
would sell for the millions
And some eccentric
Japanese
would keep it
hidden
in a vault
in Tokyo
And Skeleton Indian
would chuckle about it
You know what
that Japanese does
Skeleton Indian
would say
He shows the painting
at $10,000 a look
and whispers
That's a painting
of a code talker
That's why we lost
the war
They had death
on their side
Skeleton Indian

would die laughing
from this
if he wasn't
already dead
Mona Lisa Indian
That's him
Leonardo
who's that
A code talker
Skeleton Indian
chuckles

SKELETON INDIAN WAS A NAVAJO

Skeleton Indian
was a Navajo
when he was alive
Still am
says Skeleton Indian
No difference between
a live and dead Navajo
Still Navajos
And Marilyn Monroe Indian
was Pueblo
when she was alive
Still am
says Marilyn Monroe Indian
No difference between
a live and dead Pueblo
Still Pueblos
A great nation
of the living and the dead
just like the Navajos
How is it you two
get along so well
Him being Navajo and all
I ask Marilyn
Skeleton Indian
gets angry at that
Why is everybody always
picking on the Navajos
he says
We've suffered enough
for our raiding days
Driven away from our home
by Kit Carson
Only coming back
after years of starvation
And then in modern

times
John Colley
tried to starve us
Killing off our sheep
I love the Navajos
says Marilyn
especially this one tall
skinny Navajo
All the Pueblos
love the Navajos
she adds
moving her hips sexy like
That's what I love about her
says Skeleton Indian
She's got a wild imagination

HERE COMES SKELETON

Here comes Skeleton
Indian
back to the bar
All his friends
greet him
How come we only
see you at night
someone asks him
Night's my time
he says
Everybody agrees
It's the only time
Women try to get
Skeleton Indian
to dance
and he dances
a bit
Love me honey
the women say
He lets them go
then
I can't love no one
he says
Not a woman
nor a dog
nor a flower
His honesty
drives the women
wild
They embrace
his ribs
Caress his
cheekbones
Try to nibble
on his absent

earlobes
You're sure
the hardest man
to make love to
they say
Skeleton Indian
doesn't encourage them
He's just
who he is

THERE'S NOTHING WORSE

There's nothing worse
than not being able
to fall off to sleep
That's what Skeleton Indian
says
When you think of the dead
you probably think
they have it easy
That death's like being
asleep forever
except without dreams
Don't believe it
You've spent one night
being unable to sleep
Try an eternity of it
Skeleton Indian moans

HEAD BLOWN OFF

Head blown off 3rd time
in one dream
Wasn't it bad enough
that he was always
getting his head
blown off
each night
Now it's happening
3, 4, 8 times
a night
Dreams sneak up on him
with another episode
of untimely death
And in these dreams
he's got
movie star faces
John Wayne's
Humphrey Bogart's
Rock Hudson's
to mention a few
Taking turns
getting blown off
his shoulder
And even once
Marilyn Monroe's
face
took its turn
That was the biggest shame
not only because
it was a woman's face
but because he loved
her more
than any other woman
no matter that she
had died

when he was a little boy
When he wakes up
he thinks
Who's this
who's shooting stars
in my dreams
It was bad enough
they were shooting
me
Now they're shooting
all my
idols

THAT'S JOHN COLLEY

That's John Colley
he said
I looked where
he was pointing
and only caught a flash
of something
dark
What was that,
I said
A mouse
or a rat
Neither,
he laughed
That was John Colley
I thought about this
looking
at the juniper bushes
where the rodent
had disappeared
You mean
John Collier
the Indian agent,
I finally said
That's him,
the Navajo laughed
You know
I almost didn't talk
to you
When you drove up
I sent one of my kids
to check
your license plate
and he came back
whispering
It's no Colley plate

It's then I thought
he don't work
for the government
You know John Collier
died a long time ago
I said
Don't matter
he said
The damage's done

HE WAS APPROACHED

He was approached
by the great
blue shadow
of a man
I'm from Washington
he said
How's Lincoln
the Indian asked
Dead
the blue shadow
said
Sorry to hear that
said the Indian
How long has
he been dead
But the blue shadow
didn't answer
Instead growing larger
and more ominous
The Indian got
down
on his knees
We don't have
much land left
Are you going
to take that
he said
We took it
a long time ago
the blue shadow answered
Because of our
generosity
we gave it to you
as a reservation
But now we want it

back
There's oil and
gold there
The blue shadow
kept growing larger
until it covered
all of the land
This is what's come
of Lincoln's dying
the Indian moaned
Looking around
Seeing every way
was the same
blue way
of going away
and never
coming back

WHO WAS HE

Who was he
says Skeleton Indian
A poet
says Marilyn Monroe
Indian
A poet!
Skeleton Indian
laughs
I didn't know
he was so afflicted
Poetry must have
killed him
You really think so
Marilyn frowns
I should have discouraged
him
from writing me all
those love poems
They must have
taxed
his heart
You were always
hanging out in
bars
I was lonely
and he'd come by
with his poems
We didn't do nothing
I'd just read
his poems
Love poems!
Skeleton Indian says
shaken up
If you had told me
earlier
I would have killed him
before the poetry
did

WELCOME, SAYS SKELETON

Welcome, says Skeleton
Indian to Raymundo
Welcome
Raymundo,
says Marilyn Monroe Indian
How you liking being dead,
Skeleton Indian
asks snidely
I'm at a loss for words,
Raymundo says
And you a poet!
Skeleton Indian says
amused
Ignore him, Ray
Marilyn says
He's just jealous
I told him about
the love poems
you wrote me
All this time I've
been wishing
you were here
so you could put into words
what this place is
Where Skeleton and I
have found ourselves in
I thought then I could
make sense of it all
And here you are!
Didn't you hear
what Raymundo said,
Skeleton interrupts
Poets don't know
anything more
about death
than any other
dead person

RAYMUNDO

Raymundo,
says Skeleton Indian
Stop
staring at me
Yes, you are dead
Can't you see
he's in shock,
Marilyn Monroe
Indian says
shaking
her head sadly
What I want to know,
says Skeleton Indian,
is how did he
land up
with us
with all of eternity
around us
Besides
I thought this reservation
was only for Indians
A mistake
I suppose,
says Marilyn Monroe Indian

RAYMUNDO, SAY YOU LOVE ME

Raymundo, say you love me,
says Marilyn Monroe Indian
Skeleton Indian won't mind
as long as it's just talk
Well, maybe he'll mind a little
But what could he do
about it
I've been hurt too much
by love
to play at it,
says Raymundo
Oh, come on Ray, it don't
hurt to amuse
ourselves a little bit
What else is there to do
Ever since Skeleton and I
came to this deathly
everlasting reservation
you're the only
other person
we've seen
Skeleton wasn't too happy
seeing you at first
but since you're the only
other one around
he can't complain
too much
Why are you talking
to Raymundo
like I'm not here,
Skeleton Indian says
And I do mind him
always being around
Before he came around
we found ways

of mingling
with the living
But since he's come
it's like this deathly
reservation is always with us
Marilyn nods
in agreement
Ray, how did you alienate
us
from the living
What powers
of death do you have
and why
did you bring them to us
Why don't you take them
away with you
Skeleton adds
It's not my doing
says Raymundo
I didn't wish to come here
Maybe you two
brought me here
with all your
arguing
Maybe that's what's
alienated you
from other people
I should be the one to be upset
Marilyn Monroe Indian
and Skeleton
Indian grow
deathly quiet
They realize that there's
some truth
in what Raymundo said
They don't fully understand
the truth of it
But enough

NOTE FROM THE AUTHOR

The phrase "going home away Indian" came to my mind before I even considered writing the poems in this collection.

I was driving on Cerrillos Road in Santa Fe when I saw an older Native American man staggering outside of a liquor store. "Going home away Indian" immediately came to my mind even though I had never thought of that combination of words before. I found myself remembering a poem a friend had written in the early 1970s, a poem I hadn't thought about in a long time. My friend was a heavy drinker at the time, and one night when he was drinking and feeling homesick he took a taxi back home, where he grew up, somewhere near Acoma. Not having a car, he took a taxi for a trip of about sixty miles. My friend was soon back in Albuquerque.

Not long afterward I saw a book of Fritz Scholder's paintings called *Scholder/Indians*. I felt a jolt of emotion when I opened the book and saw one of Scholder's paintings. This continued to happen as I leafed through the book. I then closed the book and wrote a poem based on the first painting I saw. During a two-month period I would open the book randomly, look at a painting, then close the book and write a poem. Usually I wrote one poem per day, but on a few occasions I wrote two or three poems.

Scholder was depicting Indians in a contemporary/expressionistic way, somewhat reminiscent of Francis Bacon with their strong figurative emotional content. Previously in American art, Native Americans had been romanticized or sentimentalized. Those paintings lacked an energy/life that for me Fritz Scholder's paintings captured.

From the beginning, the guiding light for the poems was the phrase "going home away Indian." That phrase expressed for me the angst of the Native American experience in contemporary America, especially the urban Indian experience. So I kept it as the title.

As I wrote more and more poems, a story began to develop with characters. The first character I wrote about was Skeleton Indian, partly inspired by my friend, his strength, his anger. Then came Marilyn Monroe Indian, inspired by a young Native American woman writer who came to live with my friend. I chose the persona of Marilyn Monroe not only because she was beautiful, like the young woman, but because her life was a tragic story, as was the Native American experience.

The skeletal / deathly imagery stories have their basis in the Mexican Day of the Dead. And the Mexican character and the Raymundo character (basically the same character) have some connection to me.

After *Going Home Away Indian* was published in 1990, I gave a copy of the book to a friend who had an art gallery in Taos. Hers was one of the first galleries to represent Fritz Scholder, so I thought she might find the book interesting. After she read it she said, "Fritz would love this. Send him a copy." She gave me his address in Arizona, and I sent him a copy. Soon afterward I received a small book in the mail of Fritz Scholder's poetry. No letter. But within a short time he stopped at my bookstore in Santa Fe and we had a pleasant conversation. From then on, he often stopped at my store when he was in Santa Fe.

San Fernandez Beat

(1992)

GINSBERG'S ON THE PHONE AGAIN

Ginsberg's on the phone again
calling everyone important.
I've been waiting since four
to continue our conversation
but he's been on the line
for two hours.
This isn't the famous Ginsberg,
The Allen Ginsberg, this is
a much lesser known Ginsberg.
He spends all his days
sending off poems
to magazines and generally
to anyone whose address
is handy: the phone company,
the electric company,
the credit-card company.
And even the people who
send him junk mail get poems
from Ginsberg, and he signs
them all "A. Ginsberg" because
his name is Alfred.
I asked him once, "Isn't
this kinda deceitful and
couldn't it open you up to lawsuits
considering Ginsberg is dead?"
And he said, "That's the name
I was born to. I can't use
the name I was born to?"
I just shook my head,
and I could see the futility
of saying anything. Anyway
here I am waiting two hours
to continue our conversation,
and I start making noise
to get his attention,

and he looks up and says,
"Hush, this is an important
call." "Christ! It's been
two hours," I say with an
expletive or two thrown in.
He just gives me a sad-eyed,
brown-eyed look,
and then he's back talking
into his phone as if I
don't exist. And so I leave
and slam the door behind me.
And when I'm outside, I think,
What am I so upset about?
It was my fault for waiting
for two hours. I should have
just left after a reasonable
amount of time. Besides,
I don't much care for his
company anyway.

NEXT TIME I COME TO VISIT

Next time I come to visit,
Alfred's dad is still there.
I take Alfred aside. "What's
this? The old man's moved
in with you?" "Temporarily,"
says Alfred. "He's new in
town and is waiting for some
checks to catch up with him.
Then he's moving out."
"Hello, Mr. Martinez,
cómo estás?" I say going over
to shake his hand.
"Ginsberg," he says. "It's
Ginsberg." "But the other day,"
I say, "you said it was
Martinez?" "That was the other
day," says Mr. Martinez or
I should say Mr. Ginsberg. I look
at Alfred for some assistance.
"We talked about it," says
Alfred, "and he agreed to
change his name to Ginsberg.
With him living in the same
town as me something had
to give, and I've invested
too much of my time and
reputation on this Ginsberg
name. Do you think anyone
would bother to publish
Alfred Martinez or go hear
him read? But A. Ginsberg,
that's another matter. And
since I grew my beard
I haven't heard people asking,
'Isn't Ginsberg dead?'"

MR. MARTINEZ IS QUITE A CHARACTER

Mr. Martinez is quite a character.
I'll never get used to calling him
Mr. Ginsberg. "You've really changed
your last name?" I ask. "Sí," he
says. Mr. Ginsberg I've noticed
has a great affinity for one syllable
words. "You've changed it legally
and all?" I say dubiously. "Sí,"
he responds. "Was it difficult?"
I say. "Sure, sure," he says.
"You had to get your driver's license
changed and all your credit cards
and your bank account, and with the
government, and all of that?" "Yes.
It was work," he says. "Just because
your son wanted you to?"
"He has a career," Mr. Ginsberg says.
"I've had a career. It's his turn.
I don't want to stand in my hijo's way."
"You're very understanding," I say.
"I wish I had had a dad like you.
I wish I had had a dad period
even if he had been mean and beat me
as long as he had taken me
to some ball games and fishing."
"That's right, you didn't know
your dad," says Mr. Ginsberg.
"That's right," I say. "My mom
had me to increase the welfare check."
Mr. Ginsberg looks embarrassed,
and a period of uneasy silence
intrudes between us until Alfred says,
"You know, Dad's started writing
poetry." "Is that right?" I say
looking at Mr. Ginsberg. "That's

right," he says. "What name do
you use?" I ask. "Ginsberg," he
says. "What else?" "But Alfred's
Ginsberg," I say. "I know," says
Alfred, "it's a problem, or will be
when he starts sending his
poetry out. Did I tell you? His
first name is Alfredo. But he's
always used the initial 'A.'"
"Why don't you change
your name to Carl Solomon?"
I suggest. They both look
at each other. "I like that
idea," says Alfred. "But it's
a lot of work changing your
name," Mr. Ginsberg whines.
"That's right," I say, "but
remember, it's your hijo's career."
Mr. Martinez, I mean Mr. Ginsberg,
looks a bit despondent.
"You're right," he finally says.
I turn to see a big look of relief
on Alfred's face.

"HOW DO YOU DO IT?" I ASK

"How do you do it?" I ask
Alfred. "How do you get
so many poems published?"
As if I didn't know how.
Of course he signs his poems
Ginsberg with just the
initial "A" for Alfred,
but surprisingly
no one's complaining.
And the real Ginsberg?
He's been dead a long time.
Has everybody forgotten?
Anyway, Alfred gets published,
and I have yet to get a single
poem published.
"How do you do it?"
I repeat. "What's your
secret?" And Alfred says,
"It's all in the name. You've
got the wrong name." I knew
he was going to say something
to that effect. "But you're
already using the name,"
I say. "There are plenty
of other names," says
Alfred. "There are plenty
of famous dead poets."
"Like Rimbaud or Wordsworth?"
I say. "No, no," Alfred says
impatiently. "They've been dead
too long. How about a Latin
American writer? You have
the right looks."
"Famous but dead?" I wince.
"By God, you've got it!" Alfred grins.

I suggest a few names,
but they are all fiction writers.
Alfred begins frowning
as I come up with flop after flop.
"Pablo Neruda," he finally says.
"In a funny way you've always
reminded me of Pablo Neruda."
"Hasn't he been dead too long?"
I say. "Won't people know?"
A cloud comes over Alfred's face.
I can see he's getting real tired
of showing me the ropes and all.
"Not if your poetry's great,"
Alfred finally says.
"Then they won't care."
What a burden to carry, I think
and fret over the responsibility
of having to live up
to my new name.

MR. MARTINEZ ALWAYS HAS

Mr. Martinez always has
his mouth open, and he looks
like an insect's popped into it,
and he doesn't know whether
to spit or swallow.
"Swallow," I say without thinking.
"Qué? What's that?"
says Mr. Martinez,
alias Mr. Ginsberg. *And what
is it tonight?* I think.
"You finally change your name?"
I ask. "I changed it to Ginsberg,"
he says. "I know that," I say,
"but last time I was here, there
seemed to be a problem with
that name. And I suggested
you change it to Solomon."
"Dad and I talked about it,"
says Alfred, "but he doesn't
like that name. He's decided to
stop writing poetry. That way
he can still be Ginsberg."
"Sí. That's right," says
Mr. Martinez. "Por mi hijo.
I had a career. Forty years
with the post office delivering
mail, snow and rain. It's
his chance now to get ahead."
I don't have anything to say
to that. What does it matter
to me what they want to call
themselves. "Mr. Ginsberg, spit,"
I say and both he and his son
give me perplexed looks.

ALFRED'S ON THE PHONE AGAIN

Alfred's on the phone again.
It doesn't fail.
Every time I drop by
there goes the phone.
Sometimes even before
I get a chance
to sit down.
"Why don't you get
an answering machine?"
I ask Alfred. "That way
we don't get interrupted
all the time."
But not Alfred.
He can't resist
picking up the phone.
"A. Ginsberg here," he says,
or "Ginsberg speaking."
He claims to get calls
from all the Beat poets
living and dead.
"Dead!" I exclaim,
"How did they get
your number?"
"Probably the telephone book
or information," Alfred smiles
innocently.
When they call
like Kerouac did
the other day,
he doesn't want
to miss the opportunity.
Like Alfred says,
"Dead Beat poets
don't like to talk
to recording devices."

So oftentimes
we don't get to say
more than a few words
before the phone
starts ringing
and Alfred says, "Yeah,
uh-huh, yes, oh certainly.
You saw that poem where?
No. I didn't plagiarize you.
There are similarities
I agree.
But that has more to do
with the commonality
of the Beat experience."
That sort of thing
over and over.
Mostly he's listening,
getting writing advice.
And sometimes
I hang around
poking through
his bookshelves
adding to my literary education
that way.
But when I see him lighting up
his third cigarette,
I call it quits
and leave.

ALFRED, IF I DON'T FIND HIM

Alfred, if I don't find him
in his apartment, I can find him
at the Café Tristeza. It's not
too crowded in the daytime,
and that's when he likes to go
there by himself and smoke
and drink coffee and write
poems. I'll sit down at his table
and order coffee and not
say a word until he's finished
writing his poem which he's
always doing when I come by.
He must write three to seven
poems each time he comes to
the Café Tristeza. And when
he's through, he looks up at me
and smiles. "How long you've
been here?" he'll say. "Not
too long," I'll say no matter
how long I've been there.
"You write a great poem?"
I always ask. And Alfred
will get pensive. "It's hard
to say," he'll finally answer.
"They all look great after
I've written them." I can
understand that and nod.
But I never ask to read the poems.
I know Alfred will read them
to me some night soon enough.
And I must admit, he's getting
to be a better writer than I
ever thought he could be.
Or maybe I'm coming to appreciate
poetry more. I can actually

sit and listen to him for a half hour
and enjoy it. That is, if I have
some wine to drink. But a
half hour is tops. If he goes
on for longer than that, I
turn on the TV and watch
the cable news or the cable
weather. And Alfred gets
the message and stops reading.
Then I turn off the television.
But invariably the damn phone
starts ringing, and then I
better leave because it's
always an important call,
and he could be on the line
for hours. But at the Café
Tristeza no one calls him.
And we talk until he feels
a poem coming on.
Then he'll stop
in midsentence.
And as if I'm no longer
there, he'll start
writing on a napkin, his
favorite writing material
at the Café Tristeza.

I DROP IN ON ALFRED

I drop in on Alfred
We start talking, and as always
the telephone starts ringing.
We grow quiet, let it ring
until the machine comes on.
"Leave a brief message
after the beep,"
says Alfred's voice sounding
peculiar on the machine. He's
trying to avoid calls from
the dead Beat writers who've
been calling him for months.
They've become abusive
calling him at all hours
of the day and night
accusing him of plagiarizing.
Alfred knows they hate
answering machines and won't
leave a message afraid
their spirits will get trapped
inside the machine. We hold
our breath as a voice comes on.
"Francisco? This is your dad.
Pick up if you're there."
I stare at Alfred: *Francisco?*
"I guess you're not home.
You didn't pick up.
You haven't picked up all day.
I guess you're still out.
Why did you kick me out
of your home, mi hijo?
I stopped writing poetry
didn't I? For Christ's sake
tell me what I did wrong.
I thought we were hitting

if off. I wanted to make up
for all the years I wasn't there.
After I left you and your mom."
Another pause. "Francisco, I—"
The machine cuts off.
Alfred gets up and disconnects
the telephone.
"That's the sixth time
he's called me today."
Alfred grimaces.
"Yes! My name use to
be Francisco. Get that
shit-eating grin off your face."
"I thought you two were getting
along so well after he stopped
writing poetry," I say unable
to keep from grinning.
Alfred shoots me a hard look.
"I don't want to talk about it."
After a brief silence, he goes
to his desk and hands me
a typed poem. "Wrote it today,"
Alfred says. I read it out loud
which Alfred likes me to do.
"Dead in Florida, Kerouac. What
were you doing there? Searching
for alligator death? You were
still too young to be retiring
to Florida. Today's October 21,
and I'm thinking this is the day
on which you died. And here
I'm staring at this pumpkin on
my windowsill, all its insides
scooped out and thrown away.
And its eyes and nose and mouth
cut out and empty. The face
of death, I think, Kerouac's face
now long gone to emptiness."

I stop reading. I've reached
the end of the poem. "It doesn't
seem finished," I say. Alfred
nods. "Yeah, it's not finished,
but I'm gonna leave it like that."
I give him back the poem.
"I like it the way it is," I say.
He nods again but doesn't
say anything. "You know if you
feel like writing just kick me
out," I say thinking Alfred
wants company and won't
tell me to leave. He goes
and opens the door. "Good-bye,
Pablo," he says. That's the name
he's given me, Pablo Neruda,
to help me with my writing
career. Though people don't
seem to be taking to it too well.
I didn't expect to be leaving
so soon, but I understand the
needs of the writer. So I go home
and return to my 1,000-page poem.
I have 160 pages written so far.
Only 840 to go. And at 10 pages
a day, it'll be finished in 12
more weeks.

AS POETS GET OLDER THEY

"As poets get older they
get it in their heads
they need to live by the ocean
or out in the desert.
And they worry they're
going to run out
of new thoughts.
They pontificate
awhile
and then clam up
afraid of the dream
where they wake up
in a white gown.
1) Died and gone to heaven?
2) Joined a religious order?
3) In the hospital for surgery?
All the possibilities
frighten them."
Alfred reaches over
and scratches the head
of his old dog making
his dog blissfully happy.
"Oh, to be old and so
easily contented,"
Alfred laments.

I'M INVITED

I'm invited
to give a poetry reading
at a cafe,
but no one shows up.
Not even Alfred
who's encouraged
me as a poet
and recommended me
for the reading.
I wait nearly an hour
before leaving.
Not even the sponsors
of the poetry reading
show up.
And the employees
at the cafe
whisper
to each other,
and they look just
as embarrassed as I feel
which makes me feel worse.
It's my first and last
poetry reading I vow
as I walk through
crowded sidewalks.
All these people
and not one of them
wanted to hear me read!
I think in dismay.
Finally I stop
at another cafe
where the employees
don't know,
and so can't share,
my embarrassment.

I order a cinnamon roll
swimming in butter
and coffee even though
I know the coffee
will keep me up all night.
Thinking of the poetry
I didn't get to read,
I feel a wave of spiritual
nausea.
I eat my cinnamon roll
with little interest
and wonder
what is left to do
on such an inauspicious
night.

I KEEP WONDERING WHEN FULGENZI

I keep wondering when Fulgenzi
is going to publish my book. He's
had the poems for six months. I
meet him at Diana's Cafe.
Fulgenzi has my manuscript
with him. "We need to make some
changes," says Fulgenzi leafing
through the manuscript and scowling
at certain pages. "Changes?" I gasp
and reflexively bring a hand to
my chest as if to protect my heart.
"What kinda changes?" I feel worse
than when I went to the dentist
to have a tooth pulled out, and the
tooth wouldn't come out. The
dentist pulled and pulled, and
the dental assistant looked
at me anxiously. Fulgenzi
rips out a page from my manuscript,
and I wince. "Not in front of me,"
I protest. Fulgenzi stares at me.
"This poem's no good. You gotta
be tough skinned about this sorta
thing." Fulgenzi tears out
a lot more pages. He gives me an
intent look. "The ending doesn't
work. The beginning doesn't work.
The middle doesn't work."
I don't know what to say.
Fulgenzi takes off his glasses.
He pushes what's left of my manuscript
toward me with a look of disgust.
"Does this mean you're not
publishing my manuscript?"
I say meekly. Fulgenzi scowls.

"That's right," he says.
"Alfred suggested I look at it.
And as a favor to him I thought
maybe with some changes
we could salvage the manuscript.
But I can see now I was
being way too optimistic."
"You have any suggestions?" I say,
my lips trembling, my voice cracking.
"About what?" says Fulgenzi.
"Making changes to it, sending it
out to someone else." Fulgenzi
looks at me impatiently.
"You weren't listening to me.
I'll be honest with you.
I think you should take it out
into the country and bury it
before it stinks up this town."
I'm shocked. I hadn't expected
such frank brutality. I'm speechless.
"You really think you're doing
the right thing trying to be a writer?"
"Yes," I say weakly. Fulgenzi
turns around to shake the hand
of someone who's come up
to talk with him. Fulgenzi's grinning.
I don't exist for him anymore.
I gather my ripped-up manuscript
and leave the cafe.
The sidewalks are crowded.
Motorists are waving or honking
at some of the pedestrians.
I pick up some cheap red wine
on my way home determined
to get good and drunk. But
once I get home, I change my mind.
I fill a grocery bag with all the poems
scattered about my place.

It's everything I've ever written.
I go out and walk around the city
carrying the bag full of poems
uncertain what to do with them.
Finally I find myself
back at Diana's Cafe.
Alfred's there with Fulgenzi.
I place the grocery bag
in the middle of their table.
"You've been shopping?" Alfred says.
"These are my poems," I say
to Fulgenzi, my voice quavering,
my whole body trembling.
Alfred gives Fulgenzi a questioning look.
"I gave him my professional opinion."
"He said my poems stink
like something dead.
He said I should bury them
in the country before
they stink up the town."
"You didn't?" Alfred chides Fulgenzi.
"If he can't take criticism, he
doesn't have any business
being a poet. You know how it is.
Poets don't get a lot of respect
in the world. If you got thin skin,
you're not gonna survive."
Alfred thinks for a minute.
"Fulgenzi's right, Antonio. I've
meant to tell you many times.
You don't take criticism well."
I pick up the grocery bag,
and without saying a word I leave.
Feeling despondent and ashamed
I think about what Alfred said.
It's true. I can't take criticism.
I decide to go back home.
After I've been there

a short while, I hear a knock.
I don't answer. After a few knocks
I hear Alfred's voice. "Maybe
he didn't come back home."
Then I hear Fulgenzi's voice.
"You can't seriously believe
he's any kind of a poet. Grade-
school kids write better poetry."
There's a pause. "I was hoping
you would see something
in his work." Alfred's sounding tired.
"I can't believe what I'm hearing.
A poet of your ability, you must
see what crap it is. He's the least
talented poet I've ever run into,
and I've run into plenty of losers."
"Hush!" Alfred says. "He could be
coming up the stairs and hear you."
"I don't care. He should keep
hearing it until it gets through
his thick skull that he's wasting
his time and other people's time.
He's one big—" "OK, OK," Alfred
says. "You've said enough."
I hear them going down the stairs.
I feel like screaming but I don't.
I place the grocery bag in the sink
and set it on fire.
What if the building
catches fire? I think. *What if*
all of San Fernandez goes
up in flames? But after an initial
big burst of flames, the fire
quickly dies down. *How pathetic,*
I think, *all that poetry gone in a flash.*
Then I think of the safety-deposit box
where I keep duplicates
of every poem I've written.

160

The building is safe, I think,
San Fernandez is safe.
That is until the next great
earthquake. But that doesn't
have anything to do with poetry.
I find that thought sobering.

ALFRED'S GETTING FAMOUS

Alfred's getting famous
having book signings,
getting phone calls from
the rich and famous.
I can hardly get close
to him anymore. There's
always someone whispering
in his ear, or Alfred is
off on another reading tour.
And he's bought a farm
where he invites
his famous friends
which he said I could visit
as soon as I publish my first
book of poetry which
I'm hoping will happen
any day now. I've lost
count of all the manuscripts
I've sent out. Though
it's discouraging to see
writers almost half my age
getting their first book published.
I go to all of Alfred's book signings
when he's in town. And when
I can get his attention, I
pull him to the side and remind
him how he was going to show
me all the ropes about the
poetry business, but we were
interrupted by his meteoric
rise in fame. Alfred always smiles
his now world-famous poet
smile looking like a young Whitman.
He has grown a long beard
and taken up with young men.

Alfred always says the same thing.
"Keep writing tirelessly. Keep
sending your poetry everywhere.
Keep believing in yourself,
and you too will be famous
one of these days."
Then he is sucked up again
into the vortex of his many fans.
And I am left alone to contemplate
his words and have come to believe
that if I do become famous,
it will not be in my lifetime.

DREAM OF OLD PERUVIAN DAYS

I dream of old Peruvian days.
I'm walking the streets and alleys
of Chan Chan city. Overhead
the Milky Way looks as crowded
as the freeways of Los Angeles.
I wonder if the king has died
for the city to be sacrificing
two hundred more men and women
who I see being led by soldiers
carrying spears and torches.
One woman calls out, "Antonio!"
giving me a beseeching look
as she passes by me. A large
falling star distracts the soldiers,
and I grab her hand and force
my way through the crowd
that is mesmerized
by the falling star. We escape
out of town and hurriedly follow
an empty road across a vast plain
with only the light of the Milky Way.
We walk for hours without
saying a word but holding
each other's hand tightly
as if it's our only contact to the world.
"Where are we going?" she
finally asks after hours of walking.
By this time the night has withdrawn,
and the glow of the sun
is rising above some trees.
I turn to look at her
for the first time since we escaped.
She's smiling at me sadly, and
I realize then that she is
one of the twin blue sisters

who sang sad songs in Portuguese
in a cheap Hollywood motel
late one winter night while
I lay awake in the next room.
"Where is your sister?" I ask her
feeling her infinite sadness.
"I am my twin sister,"
she answers quizzically.
That's when I wake up and
realize I'm not in Peru, not
even in Los Angeles but in
stale San Fernandez.
I try to go back to sleep
but unable to fall asleep
I finally get up. Another day
of going out to look for work.

I WAKE UP

I wake up
and find that
I am still myself.
I would like
to wake up
some morning
as someone else.
And not remember
who I was before.
And not remember
that I changed.
I would not be me.
I would be anyone else.
It's when I feel
most abject
that I think I'd like
to be anyone else.
But if I gave it
serious thought
I'd realize
there are plenty
of people
who I'd hate to be.
That I could be
much worse off
than I am.
I quickly put
that thought
out of my mind.
I just want change.
Want to be out
of my skin
and self.
So I try to
go back to sleep.
But even I
can only sleep
so long.

ALFRED'S TURNED ARTIST, NOT

Alfred's turned artist, not
just giving readings anymore
but doing shows of his drawings
and paintings in places like
Palm Springs and Denver. I pick
up the Sunday paper and there's
a big photo of Alfred in the
Arts page. His first show
in San Fernandez. I read
all this garbage he's feeding
the Arts writer. How he sees
pencils and brushes as being
synonymous to the keys on his
typewriter. So before he
draws, he has 26 pencils laid
out or if he's painting he
has 26 brushes laid out. And
it's constant interchanging
of pencils or brushes just
like he was typing away at
a poem. And there is more stuff
and worse stuff that he
says about art and writing.
And I grimace and think,
What a phony!
But I am impressed and
amazed by his success
once again.
So I go to the art opening
and Alfred is late,
so late that people
are whispering maybe
he won't show up
because of how long it's taken
San Fernandez to recognize him

not just as a major poet
but also as a major artist.
As I'm standing
near the outside door
wondering if I should leave,
Alfred suddenly comes in
with his entourage.
The crowd parts like the Red Sea.
I'm startled and find myself
shook up seeing him in the flesh
after so long. "It's good work!"
I call out wanting him to notice me.
But Alfred doesn't look at me.
He's focused straight ahead
intent on making his
way through the crowd.
I think of what Alfred brusquely
said as he went by me,
"I haven't seen the show yet!"
There was no eye contact, and
no indication he recognized my voice.
Before I can say anything else
a wall of people closes behind him.
He doesn't know who I am anymore,
I think dejectedly and wonder
if I ever really knew him. Could it
have been some stupid dream? Then
I notice someone waving at me
like crazy. Smiling and waving.
She doesn't look familiar.
I look behind me to see who
she's waving at, but no one
is reacting to her. So I look back at her
and she's still waving and smiling
in my direction. I point at myself
with a questioning look, and she
nods yes, and shouts something
I can't hear with the noise of the crowd.

I'm certain she's not anyone I know.
She's mistaking me for someone else,
I think and that thought upsets me.
I turn wanting nothing more than
to get out of there, but the rush
of people pouring into the gallery
pushes me farther into the room
and toward the waving woman.

NOTE FROM THE AUTHOR

The poems in *San Fernandez Beat* came about after I looked through a book called *Cafe Society: Photographs and Poetry From San Francisco's North Beach.* The photographs were mainly of Beat writers in their North Beach hangouts. But there were also some photographs of locals who had nothing to do with the Beat scene. In one of those photographs, titled *Mario and Friends, Bohemian Cigar Store, 1973,* I was startled to see my uncle Margarito (Maggie) with an arm (a cigar between two fingers) around Mario's shoulder, both of them wearing suits. He and his wife, Alice, had moved to San Francisco in the fifties.

My uncle wasn't interested in literature of any kind, so I'm sure he didn't give Beat writers much of a thought. But if he wasn't interested in Beat writers, I was, and that photograph opened for me a door to the North Beach of the 1970s. Through my uncle, I felt connected to that place and time. For me, *San Fernandez Beat* became a Mexican American take on / parody of the Beat movement.

After I finished the collection, I sent a copy to City Lights Bookstore, since the owner, Lawrence Ferlinghetti, had published a number of Beat writers, and I thought he might find the collection amusing. I soon heard from his co-editor that they didn't publish anything that was too self-referential. A few months later, I happened to be in San Francisco and stopped at City Lights Bookstore. Much to my surprise, a copy of my book *Celso,* published maybe seven years before, was on display.

Some years later, my aunt Alice was visiting in Albuquerque and I went to see her. I took *Cafe Society* with me to give her. Margarito had died some years before, and I was sure she was unaware of the book.

"I didn't know my uncle liked to smoke cigars," I said. "Oh, he never smoked cigars," she said, surprised that I would say such a thing.

I then opened the book and showed her the photograph. She was astonished but glad to have the book.

Beyond Nageezi

1.

I HAVE COME A LONG WAY

I have come a long way
lured by the silence
and desolation
of the desert
to hold counsel
with the cactus

But they will not speak
and I am weary
of chewing on stones
as if they were
loaves of bread

To all horizons
exists nothing
but cactus

Hordes of cactus

Taciturn cactus
too proud to speak

I have cast my net
among the cactus
and drawn it back empty

I am not he who will lead them
I have no power to make
water spring out of these rocks

Nor to make the mute speak

Nor the blind see

DATURA

Drive to the desert
Seek water
Nearby you will find the datura
Sacred flowers
Western jimsonweed

I have come after visions,
you will sing
After poems

The sun will accompany you
with the music of its burning
You will sing

Oh old man
your face is dying in the west
Your hair flails on the straight line
of the horizon
You will sing

Oh old man
you rose naked out of the east
Out of the lake of the morning
The womanly earth moaned
Brown thighs wet with dew
Buttocks of solid granite
You will sing

The blue flute player
plays the tune of the evening
Dusk falls everywhere like dust
Stars fill the sky like ants

Beside you large flowers
whirl open
When you leave
every rock will rise like a mountain
Grass blades swishing like swords

I WANDER IN THE DESERT

I wander in the desert
across vast desolate stretches
To the east and west
bounded by arid mountains

I pick up a sun-bleached bone
and think of the heart
and brain long gone

The feel of the sun
makes no difference to it now

A giant centipede crawls
past my boot

I see where a snake slid
over the sand

A lizard gives me a wary glance
before it disappears
into a thorny thicket

There are ponderous
black beetles
unafraid of anything

Wearily I walk back to the car
after a long day of walking
in the sun

In centuries past
men came to the desert
to converse with God

They ate what crawled
over the desert floor

I haven't the stomach for it

I HESITATE BEFORE A SEVERED

I hesitate before a severed
coyote leg
and with my boot
I turn over bits of rabbit fur

Dried yucca stalks
are tall sentinels

Their stunted branches
almost bare
but for a few dark pods

The pods have long since opened
Their weathered husks remain
Like strange-looking desert creatures

A thicket contains
large stiff thorns
and a praying mantis
the length of my hand

So much that grows here
is linear or angular

Branches with few leaves

Everywhere the sparseness
of a quick sketch

A few drops of rain
begin to fall
forming little craters
in the parched sand

The clouds quickly disperse

Startled, I turn around
But it is only the sun
breaking through gray clouds

Casting a red light
over the desert

EACH SECOND LENGTHENS THE

DISTANCE

You left only two hours ago
on your five-hour drive
Already it is dark and getting cold
I think of you alone in your car
The weak headlights fending off the darkness
The tiny lights of other cars like fireflies

Tonight I think of the miles between towns
in the desert and how each second
lengthens the distance between us
And how each mile you leave behind
is so much more emptiness to deal with

THE CACTUS HAVE TAKEN STEPS

The cactus have taken steps
toward their destruction
They have begun to communicate
in convoluted language

The sky has taken hold of its skin
and ripped it off
Pearls of blood are dripping
onto the outstretched palms of the mountains

The white rocks have grown wings
and flown away like gulls
Fish are flopping in the sands
alerting the horizon with their screams

I WALK OUT INTO THE DESERT

I walk out into the desert
during the hottest part of the day
Nothing moving
Not even the slightest breeze
to stir the mesquite branches

Everything stiff and pointed
as if it would hurt to move

I think of the madmen of the Bible,
saints, wandering the deserts

Eating locusts and seeds
Relentlessly tracking down visions
Startling them out of thickets
by making a great racket

Whacking a stick against
every small bush
Kicking over stones
Surprising scorpions and crickets

I reflect on all this and stand still
as if I were one of the desert plants
Or one of the stones
scattered for miles
Casting no shadow

FLOWERS BLOOMING

Flowers blooming
out of the asphalt
next to the curb

Just out of the reach
of passing cars and feet

Two desert plants
One tall with white blossoms
The other bushy
with purple blossoms

Looking out my window
I see lots of apartments
But these are
the only flowers

It is spring
and tiny plants
are breaking
asphalt and concrete

I feel heartened
seeing those conspirators
at work

I share their secret
with them

Millions of them
across the West
working patiently

I MOVED TO THE DESERT

So I moved to the desert
Cactus in the front yard
At night when I would
read in bed unable to sleep
because of the heat
out of the corners of my eyes
I would see trails of ants
crawling up the walls
and across the ceiling

I had moved as far away
as I could but I still
had visitors
A woman who wanted to go
dancing all night
and then go sleep in the desert
I tried to explain about
the giant centipedes
and other indescribable
creatures that I had seen
one night when I had turned on
a flashlight for a few seconds

And others who came to drink
tequila until they couldn't stand
And finally a woman who spent
her last money on a tank of gas
and came to stay

I had moved to the desert
but it was not far enough away
Later when I moved to the vastness
of the plains people would write
and say, You have moved to
the end of the world
and they would wonder why

SHE PICKED THE CACTUS

She picked the cactus
spines out of my hand
while her girlfriend
waited in the car
It was the last time
she visited me,
that long drive
from Albuquerque
A short time later
I drove east over
the Sacramento Mountains
in a rain that was
verging on snow
My heater broken
and only one windshield
wiper working right
Heading for the
Llano Estacado
and three years
as a bureaucrat
A place without a river
If I could have seen
what was ahead of me
I probably would have
headed anywhere else—
No, that's not true
I was disillusioned
and hungry

2.

BETWEEN YESO AND FORT SUMNER

I think of the jackrabbits
I saw one night
between Yeso and Fort Sumner

They were lined up
along the highway
I counted over twenty
in a span of minutes

During the day
you wouldn't think
there was a living thing
for a hundred miles

Most of the jackrabbits froze
like convicts
as the headlights
swept over them

I still see them
Tense and on the verge
of bolting blindly
into the lights

CLOVIS

It was built by the railroad
It was the first time
I had lived in a town
where there was no river

Weekends Tricia and I
would pick one of countless
dirt roads that spread out
into the plains

We would drive slowly
listening to a country music
station

We seldom saw anyone else

There was little to look at
but much to think about

My job as a bureaucrat
at what seemed
like the end of the world

Tricia getting sick at nursing
school and quitting
Taking a job as a waitress

The man dying of cancer
living with his wife
in a lone farmhouse
beaten to death by burglars

The young man who shot
himself by his tractor
out in a field, under
a mercilessly clear sky
Another day of no rain

The man who was sleeping
in the room behind
his liquor store
when the gas line exploded

I had stopped there one Sunday
on the way back to Clovis
from Albuquerque

It was the only liquor store
for miles and the only one
I knew of that sold beer on
Sundays, you knocked
on the drive-up window and waited

END OF THE COLUMBUS DAY WEEKEND

It began in the mountains
coming down a winding
canyon road, ten miles
at a snail's pace, elk hunters
in front of me and behind me
Everyone wanting to pass
and dusk growing thicker
Two hundred and fifty miles
to reach home and work
the next morning, and two
hundred of those miles
across the darkening plains

Traveling nonstop
until Santa Rosa, getting nothing
on the radio but Christian stations
and static, cussing people
who won't dim their lights

Lights seen far ahead
rising and disappearing
Growing brighter like balls
of fire, a dance of witches
I drive carefully
wary of what the car lights
may suddenly reveal, that creature
half man, half coyote
causing cars to swerve
off the road without warning

All the darkness of the plains
makes me think of death and love

And I think I sense a little
of the fear my grandmother
must have felt when she died
The letting go and drifting
in the dark—and I think I hear her
calling out to me
saying, "No, no me gusta,"
I don't like it

She is communicating her fear
which she must share with someone
And these two months since she died
and never really was dead
because I didn't share it with her
Didn't die a little with her

When she was dying
they had to tie her to the hospital bed
because she kept wanting to leave it
And she kept saying in Spanish,
"Get these witches from me!"

The restaurant where
I stop to eat in Santa Rosa
reminds me of a fake front
on a Hollywood movie studio
The waitress who takes my order
doesn't return, and the gas station
where I stop at the end of town
is attended by a young girl
watching television
indifferent to me or my money

All the way to Clovis I count
the dark spots on the highway
that once were rabbits

And I think of love, how frightening,

like the death of all these rabbits
I think of the dark side of love
and how its pain can seem
as endless as the darkness of the plains

And how terrible it is to be caught
by love, a love like the one
these rabbits knew, a love
that demands everything, a quick
burst of light and a speeding wheel
How terrible is the darkest side
of love that will not let you go

FOR MILES THERE IS NOTHING

For miles there is nothing
but this house
surrounded by a few trees
and everywhere around
and beyond are fields of corn
and wheat

Giant sprinklers on wheels
move across the land
by their own power
covering the air with silver drops
of water which huge engines
have pumped from underground

We travel for hours
on dirt roads that are
left off most maps
until up ahead
we see a sign, Earth, Texas
John Deere equipment, pickups, reapers
Computerized tractors
placing a single seed at equal
distances in even rows

SLOWER THAN ANYTHING

Slower than anything
is the turtle or so
it seems as they march
suicidally across the highway
when they have the endless
plains over which to wander
I grow to recognize them quickly
A lump on the road ahead
Like a stone or a clod of mud
I try not to run over them
remembering others on their backs
or with shell broken
A liquid staining the asphalt
Turtles don't scream
Anyway, I've never heard them
Some of them die slowly
Draw their heads into their shells
While high overhead the large birds
of the vast plains gather

WHAT WAS THERE TO DO ON THE PLAINS

1.

Drink beer, drive 90 miles per hour
Drive down dirt roads without signs
Crisscrossing New Mexico and Texas
all night, through corn fields
Onion fields, peanut fields
Somewhere during the night
find a large tin building called
La Estrellita, attracting people
from the small towns of West Texas
Bovina, Friona, Hereford, Muleshoe
who work in the fields and slaughter
houses, to dance to Mexican music
Cumbias, polkas, rancheras
Stars blurry, and sometime after
sunrise driving into a small town
called Earth, getting our bearings
and heading back to Clovis

2.

Drive two hundred miles at night
to get back to family, to the mountains,
for the weekend, that's what Val
did every Friday night, drank one
to two six-packs on the way
Hardly ever saw another car
but worried a police car would stop him
And then one Tuesday he was so
fed up with work and the plains
that he left that night
He was going to call in sick
the next morning, but somewhere
before San Jon he smashed into
the back of an unlit trailer rig that had
just pulled onto the highway
from a side road

3.

Run over turtles day and night
without meaning to, run over
jackrabbits without meaning to
Buy a large turquoise-colored belt
and have your last name put on it
Marvel at the immense skies

Watch the sun set over the wheat fields
Count telephone poles from Yeso to Vaughn

4.

Go necking with women who
would like to get married
and never call them up again
Try to remember what planet you're on
Distances so great only
an astronomer would feel
comfortable with them

TONIGHT THE MOON IS LOST

Tonight the moon is lost
and the world is all darkness
I think it will never appear again
Perhaps it has wandered too far
Perhaps it grew tired of the same old routine

There were nights when I would do nothing
but watch the moon
rise over rooftops and tree branches
and I felt secure in the constancy
of the heavenly bodies

Now I have grown wiser
but no happier
knowing that all things come to an end

And darkest of all is love
Somehow it went astray tonight
For some reason that orb of light
decided to call it quits
Mend its old ways, do something different

There's nothing new under the sun
but the moon plays by different rules
Tonight it's changed its course
and fills another heart

WE LOOKED UNDER THE SOFA CUSHIONS

We looked under the sofa cushions
for change to buy discounted bread
What else do I remember
She wanted me to beat up a guy
who was spending too much time
at a phone booth where she
wanted to make a call
She left on Thanksgiving afternoon
when I was out of the house
No note, I drove all over town
all night long and left the
lights on until dawn

What else is there to remember
There should be pleasanter memories
Her coming back, that was always pleasant
Her face beaming, desiring
The desert, the plains, the city
What do I remember about the desert
Making love in the hot afternoon
Outside the window, outside the door
the cactus grown tall by the side
of the house, And the plains
The barbed wire, the broken cornstalks
Long nights spent drinking beer
Searching for tin-building dance halls
past onion fields and peanut fields
And the city? Beautiful from a distance
Luring you and ensnaring you
like a spider's web

We had so many hard times
we could have spent a lifetime
recalling them, if there had
been a time after, if something
had followed what became nothing

YOU LOVED TO DANCE

You loved to dance
I'm sure you still do
We went to dark places
and drank tequila sunrises

After the long week
everything was suspended
in that local bar
It was dank
and probably dirty
We didn't notice much

We danced sometimes
more drunk than not

And in twenty-some years
I've only been back there once

Have you been back there?

Probably only once too,
if at all

Like me you probably passed
through there on your way
to somewhere else

WALTZING

We were waltzing once
so long ago in Clovis

Dancing at the end of
town
At the Copper Penny

It had been a waltz of sorts
getting together,
being there in Clovis

"The end of the world,"
a friend wrote to me
"That's where
you are"

Where we were

There are fields
of sunflowers
at the end of the world

And such immense
skies

Of course you
would expect that
at the end of the world

Waltzing

A man and a woman,
what better thing
can they do than waltz

Waltz to the end
of the world as we did

Looked over the edge?

Did we dare?

We didn't

3.

AT NIGHT THESE

At night these
beautifully sculpted hills
seem near even in their
charcoal darkness, They
are like wild animals that
draw near to human habitations
while people sleep, Beyond
the silhouettes of these
rounded hills is the faint
glow of Albuquerque

Encased in metal and glass,
speeding at sixty miles per hour,
I feel helpless, I look away
from the weak headlights for
a moment and toward the dim
stars and wonder how many
of those stars may have long
ago burned out and yet
their light keeps traveling

I think of the dusk of that
one early evening when my car
was struck by a truck, The car
seemed to turn slowly and heavily
with the impact though it all
happened fast, My body was
brutally tugged in opposite directions

Everything came to a crashing halt
But something within me kept traveling
like those lights of distant stars

THERE IS AN ANCIENT BELIEF

There is an ancient belief
that the moon is a way station
for the souls of the dead
on their way to heaven
To becoming stars

And for me driving on this early
snowy morning along
the length of the mountain
there is no way station ahead
unless it's the convenience store
for coffee and gas

No stars to aim for
Only another day at work

I CLIMBED A HIGH HILL

I climbed a high hill
Half as high as the canyon's rim
And heard a cacophony of birdcalls
from a hidden ravine

It was only a short while
before I saw the first
screeching blue jays
flying close to the ground
in between the junipers
They passed close to where I sat
resting behind a small tree

Swooping inches from the ground
they suddenly lurched into the sky
as the hill dropped off precipitously
leaving them deliriously high

Where I lost sight of them
in the panorama of ravines and hills
Their distant screeching
sounding like intoxicated laughter

I STEPPED OUTSIDE

I stepped outside
into the crisp October air
drawn out by the sound of drums

I sat on the hood of my car
enjoying the fall night

There is a football game
at Taos High School
The sounds carried over
many dark fields and a dense
growth of trees

I heard the cries of many voices
sounding nearer than they were

Sudden outbursts
in the moonless night
of triumph and dismay

WALKING DOWN

Walking down
the dirt road
I'm preoccupied
with thinking
how long
my money will last

I pass by houses
at the Wurlitzer Foundation
where other artists
and writers
are worrying about money

Several of them
have had to get food stamps

I feel fortunate
I'm not that bad off yet
I can't imagine
walking into
the Taos welfare office
and applying

I grew up in that
sort of poverty
and thought I had
left it far behind me

The trees
that line the road
strain in a sudden wind
Brittle leaves
are ripped
from their branches

Fluffy seeds rise up
from the weedy fields
and swirl away

A light rain
begins to fall
It feels like
it could snow soon

The weather's
sudden change
has caught me
unprepared

The wind pierces
my thin jacket

I stand for a few minutes
getting wet and cold
Partially I can see
Taos Mountain
above the trees

I can't remember
where I was heading
I think about a poem
I've been trying to write
where I kill off a character
I've been writing about for years

But the character is
refusing to die
So far I've only managed
to kill a priest

Celso was supposed
to have come along
a river
drunk
Fall in and drown

Where did the priest come from?

Never one to miss an opportunity
Celso marked off the section
of the bank where the priest
fell into the river
and began selling holy water
claiming that part of the river
where the priest fell in
was now holy

It seems to me that Celso
is having fun with me

"If I can't kill him off
I'll stop writing about him,"
I decide
See how he likes that
Leave him in limbo

I turn around
and head back home
thinking of starting
my first fire
in the corner fireplace

Then I remember
why I had gone out
And start gathering
broken branches
to make a fire

SPIDERS SCURRY

Spiders scurry
as I take
some wood from
the woodpile

As soon as the wood
catches fire
in the fireplace
I return outside
to smell the smoke
of the piñon wood
in the crisp air

The sky is darkening

I walk away
from the house
through the tall
dried weeds
scattering seeds
as I go

I look back
across the field
through the
growing dusk
and think how
there is no one home

Only a wisp
of rising smoke

A FEW HEAVY RAINDROPS

A few heavy raindrops
splatter on my windshield
Then the rain holds off
Maybe changing to snow
high above

I park alongside a rural road
and watch the trees,
their slender, stark
branches turning dark

A car drives past me slowly
with headlights on
going in the direction
of Villanueva, the last village
at the end of this winding road

Across a meadow
the Pecos River is running low

I start up my car
and drive slowly
past fields fading
into deep shadows

As I go around a bend
a browsing horse
in a meadow snorts

Startled and annoyed
as my headlights
suddenly draw him out
for an instant

4.

IN THE LATE AFTERNOON

In the late afternoon
I walked to a small restaurant

I stopped outside the window
and looked in
at the small tables
Most of them empty

I could see people
walking behind me
in the reflection of the window

Traffic was passing behind me
Neon lights were coming on

I had one of those feelings
where I wondered if I was alive

I turned around and walked
back home feeling
a few biting drops of cold rain

A flock of small birds
burst out of some
darkening trees

I OPENED MY WINDOW

I opened my window
to let in the cool air
and the smell of rain

A soothing breeze parts
the warm air in my room
and bathes me, caresses me
like oil massaged over my skin

I am refreshed
Sitting before my window
Seeing the gray sky through branches
Enjoying the company of a rain-swept day

I know others have said
that I am living alone
But that's not true, I live
with my window open to the world

CLOUDS ARE MOVING

Clouds are moving
down the mountains
like a furious glacier

The trees seem heavier,
more poised,
more steadfast

This autumn weather
revives me

No undue heart tremors
No yearnings

Just a quiet repose

Through my open window
I see a bird glide
out of the grayness
of the sky

Into the shelter of trees

THE WIND IS KNOCKING

All night I listen
to the crickets
outside my bedroom window

They do their best
to serenade me
but though I'm tired
I cannot sleep

All night I listen
to the wind
which has been blowing
for days

A few hours
before dawn
I try listening
only to the crickets

But the wind
is knocking on the roof
The trees are straining

And dust accumulates
on the windowsills

WINTER HAS ARRIVED

The long grasses tremble
in a steady breeze

Young girls wearing jackets
huddle as if discussing
this sudden change of weather

And then they disperse
like windblown leaves

Hair flailing
Purses dangling

Overhead the wintry clouds
take position on mountaintops
like an invading army

Reconnoitering
before moving down

AFTER THE SUN SETS

After the sun sets
I sit by the window
and watch the darkening
of the pine trees

Finally the wind has stopped
blowing and I can think
without feeling stressed

I can think of these trees
after sunset,
their tranquil, darkening shapes
Earlier I cursed the wind
as I walked against it
all the way home

The wind unnerves me,
breaks my words
so they have sharp edges

I am wondering
what I can say to you
and wish I could send you
the darkening of trees

How calmly they slip
into the darkness

If I could send you this,
I would send you
something of me

How branches link into shadows
and join night

I FOLLOW DARK WINTER BIRDS

I follow dark winter birds
down an arroyo

They keep a short distance
ahead of me
foraging in places
clear of snow

Large snowflakes crash
against my eyeglasses

Beyond the canyon's opening
clouds have parted
revealing
an orange-and-red smudge
where the sun set

I retrace my steps
no longer seeing any
of the tiny winter birds
I had been following

The darkening shapes
of juniper and piñon
flit across the ground
disappearing in the dusk
and the falling snow

I hurry toward the car
A nighthawk swoops
over my head

Branches crack
Rocks overturn
Darkness clings to me
like cobwebs

SCRAPING OFF THE ICE

Scraping off the ice
from my car windows
I think of pine boughs
bent with snow

Driving to work I see
the ravens camped
in the middle
of the snow-covered road

There is a casualness
about them that I like
How they wait until
the last instant
to give me the road

Grayish-white clouds
descend and break open
Piñatas covering the world
with enormous snowflakes

MOON AND RIVER

Seeing the moon
reflected in the river
I am reminded
of who we are

We know that what
we are seeing
is only a reflection
We know that the river and moon
are many thousands of miles apart

And yet we see them as one
Nothing in nature is changed
by this occurrence
Except we notice

And I am reminded
of who we are
Transient, shimmering light
within a body

5.

DRAWING UP THE BLINDS

Drawing up the blinds
I see a partial moon
in the west
Almost half a moon
An orange tinge

The moon's glow
casts shadows of the trees
on the blinds

I'd rather be asleep
than awake
looking out the window
at a partial
winter's moon

I had been hoping
to be sleeping soundly tonight
but an old familiar pain
is back again
robbing me of the health
I was feeling

Sadly it had not been
very far away
Just around the corner
Waiting for a January
night
with a partial moon
with an orange tinge

I cringe thinking
how it has stayed so near
Familiarity
It owns me

YESTERDAY AS I DROVE PAST

Yesterday
as I drove past
a neglected cemetery
I thought about the people
buried there

They had families,
friends, jobs, homes
So many things
But in death all they have
is the grave they're in
And not really that

Everything is gone

Their world
Their possessions
Their life

I have nothing
but memories

SEEING YOU FROM A DISTANCE

Seeing you from a distance
I rushed toward you

But no matter how fast
I walked
I couldn't reach you

Nevertheless I kept
rushing toward you
Seeing you off at a distance
waiting to cross the street

Then a bus stopped
between us

The traffic that
had stopped
at the red light
moved on

A crowd of people
walked past
where you had been

WHEN YOU WERE LIVING

for Sarah

When you were living
in Los Alamos
you had cable TV
and could see
Burns and Allen
and Groucho Marx

I would stay a little
longer than I had planned
when those old TV
programs came on

I saw the last minutes
of a Burns and Allen
program the other night
and I thought of you

It was more than twenty
years ago that we first met
You'd come to my apartment
and we'd watch Mary
Tyler Moore
who you resembled
Single, slim, a career woman
Groundbreaking television
at the time

I remember a sadness to you
I remember you smoking
and your bad cough
What you would die from

I remember leaving
your apartment one late
night after we watched
some television

I lived a few blocks away
past many pine trees

I looked back hoping
to see you standing
in the light
of your open door
But you weren't there

I shivered not from coldness
but from sadness

My sadness stretched
across the sky
It dwarfed the forest of dark pine
that stopped at the edge
of your house

As I walked away
my sadness
became a wind
that fled
into the black pine forest
and rose into the night sky

Stars quivered
as if on the verge
of extinction

WALKING THROUGH THE FOREST

Walking through the forest
I came across a heart
It was in the deepest part
of the forest where there was
no sunlight

Rough bark to the touch
It was a heart
But having been in the forest
so long
it had grown bark
like the trees around it

So that is what protects a heart,
I thought
A heart that once knew desire
as great as an ocean

RETURNING TO LOS ALAMOS

Returning to Los Alamos
after a long time
I walk to the pond
and watch
white-breasted birds
skimming over
the rippling water

As the sun sets
I am remembering you
The setting sun
gives the pond
a bronze sheen

Overhead many birds
swoop and dive
seeming to revel
in the dying rays
of light

My thoughts settle
about me
as evening settles
about me

I am remembering you
as the world changes
to dusk

Remembering your
fragile smile
Your light touch
Your loneliness

Where have you
gone to
since you died?

White-breasted birds
swooping in and out
of the dusk

THE NIGHT PULSATES

The night pulsates
with the rhythmic crying
of the cicadas

I lie on the grass
watching the moon
rising between
the poplars

I am anchored to this earth
I think and wonder
what would happen
if I could set adrift

The hot night
surges around me

I think of going home

6.

ANOTHER COLD NIGHT

I start my letter,
"Wishing you were here"
But then I don't know
what else to say

I write the line over
and over until I reach
the bottom of the page

When I opened the bottle
of wine I told myself
it was to keep off the cold
of this fall night
But it was loneliness
that made me feel so cold

Because you are not here
I almost regret having
loved you—almost

I put aside my pen giving up
trying to write you a letter
I pour another glass of wine
shivering as I pour it

WAS IT FALL

Was it fall
when we spoke
on the phone
so long ago?

You in New York
Me in Santa Fe

I meant to say,
The leaves
have lost
their shine

The grasshoppers
have gotten groggy
with the cold weather
and jump into me
with feeble leaps

I meant to say,
In the empty lots
plants are sending
off seeds
Sailing the wind

What did I say
all those times
we spoke?
Before you moved here
and married me?

I only remember
what I didn't say

YOU'RE IN THE YARD

You're in the yard drawing
the wild grasses I planted
in the spring
I scattered the seed
Raked it into the ground

The three-day Labor Day weekend is
coming to an end
Tomorrow I return to work
and my long commute
Up early, back late

Every now and then
I have to remind myself
that I'm alive
and not a machine

You finish your drawing
and place the drawing pad
and pencils on the kitchen table

I'm drinking my second Tecate
thinking about work tomorrow
The clothes I'm washing
are on the spin cycle

I look at your drawing
of the wild grasses
and think how they are
covered with seed—
the wind their natural sower
tugs at their stalks

7.

CHACO CANYON

Flat stones
stacked to make walls
remind the living
of the past

Kivas now with the sky
for their roof

Anyone can walk in there
and see the mysteries are gone

You climb out of the canyon
and there is only desert
as far as you can see

When people left here
hundreds of years ago
were they searching
the sky for clouds?

I sift soil
through my fingers
Fine as flour

Ants are carrying
turquoise beads
out of their anthills

The blue and green stones
once glinting in the sun
now dulled
after hundreds of years
in darkness

THE MOUNTAINS CALL ME

The mountains call me
The hollow earth is drummed
by river's hands
The fields are pointing
My blood follows the hills
It leaves my tired body behind
My mind less tired
can neither walk nor fly

Abandon yourself to me
Come into me and be not solitary
See how the clouds crowd about me
How every grass blade has its place
You need not speak and I will understand
Come and you will not be forgotten

I SKIRT THE BISTI

I skirt the Bisti
Eroding badlands
Revealing dinosaur bones
Petrified wood

Pass a refinery
at Lybrook
Not much else
An elementary school
and a few trailers

And the ubiquitous pumps
drawing out
of mother earth
the liquid
and gaseous remains
of ancient life

Scattered far apart
are the solitary homes
of the Navajos

The past carries me
through this land
A tank full of it

Off the main road
countless miles
of dirt roads
fade away
to places like Kenebeto
or Kin Klishin

Places that are hardly
places
More
descriptions
of places
long abandoned

Places of windblown sand

THERE IS NO SOUND HERE

There is no sound here
but what the wind makes
going over the desert

Stones cry out
as if they were alive

Sand swirls up into
living forms
and departs

Insects leave tracks
in the sandy arroyo beds

Where are they going to?
Where did they come from?
It seems to matter here

I find that I have gone
in a circle
and have encountered
my own footprints

Immediately I am
suspicious of them
and become alert
to sudden treachery

I open my mouth to speak
But I only hear the wind
My mouth and throat
too dry to speak

I see disintegrating
chalky bones
and bits of fur

Already the wind
is covering
my footprints
that I was following

SILENCE EXISTS HERE

Silence exists here
(the tongueless one)
Walking the hills
Hiding to catch the rabbits
Waiting for the berries to ripen

Here the trees
seek to separate themselves
To be alone
in barren hills
Listening intently
for the words sharper than grass

BEYOND NAGEEZI

1.

A hundred miles
beyond Bernalillo
heading north
and then west
there is Nageezi

And beyond Nageezi
there is nothing
though there are
illusions of places

There is only Nageezi
A Navajo name
And nothing much else

2.

I say that beyond Nageezi
there is nothing
no matter
what the map shows

When I reach Nageezi
I know I have grown
immeasurably old
And that I have driven
here too fast

How could I drive
any slower to Nageezi?
Even when I let up
on the gas pedal
the speedometer
didn't show
any slowing down

3.
It turns to night
before I reach Nageezi
The headlights
reveal ghostly figures
walking along the road

By the time I reach Nageezi
I have already forgotten
my name

Was it wind?
Mountain?
Hole in the ground?

4.
When I reach Nageezi
I step out of the car
and wonder if I haven't made
a terrible mistake
coming here

The wind makes
a groaning sound
as it passes
through the emptiness
within my head

If someone were to show me
on a map that there are
places beyond Nageezi
I would rage at them
and call them mad

FOR LAME DEER (SIOUX MEDICINE MAN)

We entered a dark room
  a round dark room
All the windows were covered
and the cracks of the door
  no light entered
We sat on a ledge
against the wall

In the middle of the room
lying on the ground
was the medicine man
wrapped in a large blanket
Quickly, quickly
the wings came
brushing against us
O, the wings came
making a whir in the air
    the many voices
    the many voices!

Remember, remember
years back
when we were dancing
and the tall grass returned
The young men went hunting
and the women made their cheers
O, the steps of the spirit wind
parted the grass
and the young men followed
The hollow sun
beat like a drum
leading the men on
And when they returned
with their kill
the horizon played its flute,

an evening song
Then the fires burned
late into the morning
Ghost songs
    the many voices
    the many voices
As if waking from a dream
the wings are gone
The spirits were among us
the spirits, the spirits
To all the four corners
they have gone
Open the door
Let the sun enter
on its four feet
O, I am hanging in the air
dangling from leather thongs
My muscles are breaking
The sun is entering my brain
    O, sun my father
Your flames burn in my flesh
    O, sun
    O, father

A REMEMBERED DREAM
Thoughts on Becoming a Writer

1.

WHEN I WAS A COLLEGE STUDENT, I went to Mexico City by bus
during a school break. At El Paso, the border, I had to walk across the
bridge separating Mexico from the United States to get a Mexican bus.
When the bus pulled up to the bus station, a mob of people rushed to
it. They were packed tightly trying to board the bus, and the bus was
filling up fast. Discouraged about being able to get onto the bus before
it filled up, I backed away from the crowd. Then I saw an empty bus
pulling up behind the packed bus and got in.

I had been sleeping when I woke up to voices screaming "¡Los
niños! ¡Los niños!" The bus lights vanished into darkness. The bus
was parked on the side of the road. I soon learned that we were by the
edge of a canyon and that the bus I had tried to board in Juárez had
gone into that canyon.

2.

The earliest memory I have is of eating too many small green apples
from a tree that was either in the yard where I lived or at an adjoining
property. I remember having a stomachache from eating the unripe
apples. And afterward I remember sitting inside a darkened room.
One day my brother Ted pointed out that house while my wife and I
drove him and his wife to breakfast. It's only a couple of blocks from
where he's lived for a long time. Driving slowly, I caught a glimpse of
a very small house back from the road and partly hidden by a trailer.

How old was I at the time of that memory? I know I wasn't in school yet when my family left that neighborhood and moved to South Gonzales Street, where I became friends with Paulajean and her sister and a few other children who lived nearby. All these new friends only spoke English. I remember a number of them, though I don't remember a single child I played with in the previous neighborhood. In high school a girl told me that my mother liked dressing us up as if we were dolls. She smiled at the remembrance. This was when my family still lived where I had eaten those apples. So I was surprised by her memory, a memory of us that I had long forgotten. That made me think that over the years when she had seen me, or thought of me, it had been with the perspective of this memory of us, a richer view of me than I had of her and as such, a richer sense of the past. I only knew her from school I had thought. That made me wonder about other children I had played with back then who had totally vanished from my mind.

I think that memory of eating the green apples goes back to when I was three or four. At that point in my life, my main language was Spanish. Besides my mother and siblings speaking Spanish, I suspect that the children I came in contact with spoke Spanish because growing up I've always understood what people said when they spoke to me in Spanish. But I never felt comfortable speaking it. And, besides, if I tried to speak Spanish, the words were nowhere to be found, leaving me feeling embarrassed and making those around me uncomfortable. It was like I didn't know what those words were, though if I heard someone saying them, I understood them clearly. Though my mother and siblings spoke Spanish at home, I suspect they spent very little time speaking with me when I was little. I know that was the case when I was older. My mother, being preoccupied with my siblings, and life in general, didn't often have free time to speak with me all that much. And with our age difference, seven to ten years, there was very little contact between me and my siblings.

I once told a man that when my family moved, it seemed like I had switched from Spanish to English overnight. He said that was impossible. Of course, the change didn't happen overnight, but after we moved it happened fast. I have no memories of having had a difficult time learning English even though I got no help with English at home.

3.

Playing with neighborhood kids, and running in and out of their houses, sometimes a parent, usually the father, would ask, "¿Quién es tu papá?" *Who is your father?* was an inevitable question if they could corner me for any length of time. My solution was to run off as if I hadn't heard them. This question was so frequent that I sometimes felt that people did it intentionally to cause me pain. What could I tell them? I had no idea who my father was. I was afraid of what people might call me, think of me, and then there was the added stigma of living on welfare. Probably sometimes people asked the question innocently. Being a small community, maybe they were wondering if we could be related, or wondering if they might know my father, or some other connection. But it must have been apparent to many people what my situation was. Did they know that my mother had been divorced for a long time before I was born, that I was born out of wedlock? Or was that what they were wondering?

4.

I think I encountered my father once. I can't say I met him.

I might have been about seven years old and was at Dick's one-room grocery store looking at the penny candy in his display case. I probably didn't have any more than a few pennies to spend and was deliberating very carefully. There was a drunk man next to me who was being very annoying. I hadn't had that experience before. Drunk men usually kept their distance. He kept staring at me. Then he got very close and said something, but his words were so slurred that he was unintelligible. I had never seen him before and couldn't imagine that he was talking to me even though he kept staring at me.

When I'd be collecting empty wine bottles for their deposit, I'd catch a whiff of cheap wine, which would almost cause me to retch. I found it hard to believe that anyone would willingly drink something so nauseating.

But until that time in Dick's store, the winos had always been a presence off at a safe distance. The closest I ever came to them was when they'd see me collecting empty wine bottles, and then they'd chase after me, but in their drunken condition the chase wouldn't last very long. The empty wine bottles were what they'd collect and sell when they had no money left and were desperate for another bottle of wine.

I did my best to ignore the drunk man in Dick's store by focusing more attention on the penny candies in the glass display case. There was so much to consider. But he wouldn't leave me alone, so I finally moved away from the display case. As small as Dick's store was, there wasn't anywhere to go to get away from him. He followed me, leaving me confused as to why he was pestering me. I avoided looking at him, but he kept pushing himself in my way, so finally I looked him in the face. I quickly looked away, but the look in his eyes stayed with me for years. For a long time I didn't understand what that look meant, not consciously anyway. It wasn't until I was quite a bit older that I began making sense of that look. He was my father, and it was only because he was drunk that he had dared approach me. His eyes had tried to say to me what his drunken words were unable to express. That he knew who I was? That he was my father? Nothing more?

Sometime before this experience, my mother avoided a man who was standing in our way a short distance from where we lived, which was near Dick's store. My mother grabbed me and pulled me close to her, her face lowered as we went by him. I didn't get a good look at him, but it seemed to me that he was wanting to say something, but with my mother avoiding him, and us going by so fast, he didn't say anything. Later on, I realized that man was the man I saw in Dick's store. Had he made other attempts to try to contact us that my mother had avoided?

At the time in Dick's store, I was wanting him to leave me alone so I could concentrate on looking at the candy. Then he moved his body very close to me and at the same time turned his face away. And that's when I noticed a dollar bill sticking out of his pants pocket. Without giving it a thought, I grabbed the dollar and slipped it into my pocket. For me the dollar was a tremendous amount of money.

Stealing something was not anything I ever considered doing. But I was so annoyed by how the man kept pestering me that I took the dollar, thinking of it as my revenge for how he was treating me. It was a split-second decision, and as soon as I had the dollar, he was out the door. I immediately felt bad about having taken the dollar. I went over to Dick, who was behind the counter, and handed him the dollar. "The man who was here dropped this," I said. He took the dollar without a comment. I was expecting that Dick was going to return the dollar to the drunk man the next time he saw him. But years later, thinking of that look on Dick's face, I realized he probably kept the dollar. I suspect the man was a stranger to Dick. I was in and out of Dick's store often, rushing there whenever I had a penny or two, and sometimes when I didn't have any money just to look at the candy, and I can't recall seeing the man there at any other time.

Had my father been near the store waiting for my mother to come by, to again try to say something to her when he saw me go in the store and then followed me, emboldened by his drunkenness? Did he sometimes hang around where we lived, especially when he had been drinking?

If Dick kept the dollar, that's OK. It was a small payment for the credit my mother ran up in his store that she was never able to pay off.

5.

After I gave Dick the dollar, I went home. Without thinking of what I was saying, I blurted to my mother that I had found a dollar. But before I could explain that it belonged to a drunk man, and that I had given it to Dick so he could return it to the man the next time he came into the store, my mother grew happier than I had seen her in a long time.

She was euphoric talking about what a great time we were going to have, going to see a movie in new town and having Hershey bars. A movie ticket for an adult cost fifteen cents, Hershey bars cost a nickel. A Hershey bar with almonds was my mother's favorite treat. We had them seldom, usually only eating a small piece of the bar at a time. Finally, my mother paused long enough for me to explain that I had given the dollar to Dick so he could return it to the drunk man when he returned.

The look of happiness on my mother's face collapsed. The wonderful time she was imagining we would have vanished.

When my family lived in that small two-room extension facing South Gonzales, where we lived at the time, is when I remember some of the worst times we had trying to make ends meet. It's when I would go with my mother to a warehouse to stand in line to get commodities.

I've often thought of that dollar and that my father intended me to have it. Maybe that was part of what he was trying to say in his slurred speech, that he had a dollar for me, a present. A dollar to make up for the years of not being there. For the years of poverty. For the years of people asking, "¿Quién es tu papá?"

I'm glad I didn't keep the dollar even though my mother would have known some happiness for that day.

The rare times my siblings' father was mentioned, no one acted as if he wasn't also my father. But a look on their faces, a tone in their voices made it clear to me that he wasn't my father. That added to the distance that existed between us.

6.

I remember one time being alone with my mother and her searching for something to make for a meal. She found some old, hardened pieces of tortilla. She toasted them in a pan on the woodstove and then we spread some lard on them. A lot of the time I can remember, it was just me and my mother eating something very slight or not eating at all. I'm sure my siblings experienced plenty of those hard times too—my brother Ted has talked about it—but I hardly remember my siblings being around. Because of our age difference, it was like I grew up as an only child. I have as few memories of my siblings as I have of some relatives whom I only saw every few years.

My sister, Sara, has told me how she, Ted, and Albert would go visit our aunt María who would make them something to eat. It seems like they had ways of finding something to eat.

7.

Sometime after we moved to South Gonzales, I had a vivid dream of being carried away by the river in Chacón. The river flowed a little ways below my grandparents' house along the road.

In my dream, I was being carried away by a flooding river. There was a dead chicken floating by me, there was a plank of wood like from some outbuilding. The water was murky except for the tips of the waves. At the very tip there was a crystalline drop of water that briefly separated from the wave. I didn't feel any concern about being carried away by the water, about drowning. I was just intent on observing what was around me.

Then one day not long afterward, a cousin I didn't recognize showed up. I later learned that he was brought up by my grandparents after his mother died giving birth to him and that he was in Chacón when I was born.

My cousin was living in Wyoming with siblings and had not been back to New Mexico in several years. My mother was overjoyed to see him and introduced him to me by saying, "This is your cousin Melvin who pulled you out of the river in Chacón." It was something she had never talked about before. I was astonished. What I had thought was a dream turned out to be real.

I probably was about seven when my cousin Melvin came to visit. I never saw him again. But many years later I heard he moved to Albuquerque from Wyoming and that one day he shot himself in the head.

Recently I was in Albuquerque to see my aunt Alice, my mother's sister, who was visiting from San Francisco and staying with my aunt Katie and her daughter Lisa. I mentioned this dream and then talked about Melvin, how my mother had said he had pulled me out of the river. Alice was still living with her parents in Chacón when my mother gave birth to me. Alice said, "It was my responsibility to keep Melvin away from you. He'd go to your cradle and shake you very hard. He must have been jealous."

Lisa said, "Maybe you didn't fall into the river, maybe he pushed you in."

How old would I have been when I fell in the river? About the age I was when I ate the green apples? Maybe it's my earliest memory. A memory I had thought was a dream.

8.

When I was about nine, my grandparents took me to stay with them in Chacón. No one said anything to me about why I was going. They showed up, took me, and that was it. Then when they brought me back, there was a baby brother. I hadn't even known my mother was pregnant.

Before leaving with them, an uncle gave me a little spending money. After we were in Chacón a short time, my grandparents took me shopping with them at the only grocery store in Chacón. It was a small one-room adobe building. I spent my money on penny candies and landed up with a small bag full. In the part of the valley where my grandparents lived, close to the mountain, houses were widely scattered. There were no children to play with. And my grandparents didn't allow me to stray too far from the house. I rationed the candy to survive the time I spent with them, allowing myself two or three small candies a day. My grandparents only spoke Spanish, and I only spoke English. It was a chore trying to talk to them. When I tried to speak to them in Spanish, they weren't encouraging. Besides, they weren't into having conversations with children. Children were to be seen and not heard. I found that to be generally the way it was with other adults. I would get stern, disapproving looks when I tried to talk to them. But then they wanted me to speak to them in Spanish, not English. And perhaps my not having a father made some of the men uncomfortable. And while the women tried not to make their feelings obvious, they no doubt had similar feelings. I learned early on that men and women aren't that different except for some superficial differences.

9.

Sitting on the porch of my grandparents' house I looked with longing at the swiftly moving river. It was only a short walk down the hill. I looked at the mountains with the same longing. I was anxious to run off and explore, but my grandparents kept a close watch on me.

One day there was a plate of what I thought was crumbled cooked hamburger in the middle of the table. Earlier we had gone in the car to an isolated canyon where a man raised goats. My grandparents bought a young goat, a cabrito, and put it in the trunk. The goat kept hitting the trunk with its hooves all the way back. I was shocked when the goat was strung up by its back hooves and my grandmother slit its throat but not before a container was placed to catch the blood from its neck.

I filled my plate with what I thought was hamburger until I put a large spoonful of it in my mouth. It was the cabrito's cooked blood. I remembered its hooves kicking the trunk of the car. It tasted like liver, which I hated. When no one was looking, I spit it out in a napkin and despaired at the full plate sitting before me. My grandparents were stern, especially about eating what you put on your plate. And I didn't know the Spanish for *I don't like cooked blood*. Besides, they wouldn't have sympathized with me anyway. They grew up in a time when not much of an animal was wasted.

10.

In my fifties I asked my mother who my father was. I had never asked her before because I knew it would cause her great embarrassment, as well as me, and I suspected she wouldn't tell me.

My mother looked as embarrassed as I imagined she would be. I hated putting an old woman, my mother, in this sort of distress, but I finally felt I had to know. Silence followed, as I suspected it would.

When we were sitting at the Spic & Span restaurant, and I asked my mother who my father was, and she lowered her eyes looking embarrassed, staring at her cup of coffee, I let it go. But the next time I saw her, and took her to the Spic & Span, she waited for the coffee to arrive and then she told me a little bit about my father. Obviously, she had given it much thought since I had last seen her.

She said his name was Sam Salas. (I had my mother's maiden name, Romero.) She said that he and his cousins would come and visit her. Actually, my father's sister lived in an apartment next to my mother, and that's how my mother first got to know my father. "They liked to drink too much," my mother said, showing her disgust by making a sour-looking face. I never saw my mother take even a single drink of alcohol. "He was too young," she added. But one winter when it was extremely cold, and she didn't have money for firewood, he brought her a load of firewood. It dawned on me that I was conceived in exchange for a load of firewood. That thought bothered me at the time, and for some time afterward, but with time I've thought at least my mother and my siblings didn't freeze that winter.

Then my mother told me that she had recently been at a doctor's office and had seen some of my father's relatives there. They said that he had long ago moved to Pueblo, Colorado, and that he had died some time back. They mentioned he had a daughter who worked at a McDonald's in Pueblo. They also told her that my father's cousin named Celso had been found frozen under a bridge in Las Vegas.

I was startled to hear her story because many years before, I had written a series of poems about a character named Celso who was a borracho, a town drunk.

After my mother's story, I realized Celso must have been one of my father's cousins who came with him to visit his sister and my mother, one of those she said drank too much.

11.

One day my mother went to a dirty, run-down little store looking for credit. My mother would take me with her when she asked for credit, no doubt hoping to get the sympathies of the owners. She didn't get credit at that store, but the owner offered me a chocolate bar that was on display on a dusty shelf facing a window. When my mother and I left the store, I unwrapped the candy. I took a bite and immediately spat it out. The candy was rancid. It had probably been on display in the window for a long time. My mother laughed, her look saying, *What do you expect for free?*

12.

On a recent visit my wife and I took to Las Vegas, my brother Ted pointed to a small apartment complex, the outside walls covered with pieces of sandstone. We had been driving back to his house, after going out for breakfast with him and his wife, when Ted asked me to turn up a road a short distance from his house. "That's where you were conceived," he said, pointing to a small corner apartment.

Over the years, I had driven past that apartment complex only a few times, but it had always caught my attention because it's the only building in the area with the walls covered by a local sandstone called moss rock. Thirty years ago, I bought a tremendous amount of that stone from a relative, who delivered it to my property in Santa Fe. Over time, I've used it for making walls, walkways, etc. I've always felt something comforting about working with it.

And there Ted pointed out to me that I was conceived in an apartment with walls of that moss rock, a place I only lived in as a fetus.

At breakfast we had been talking about places where the family had lived when I was very young. I had mentioned my earliest memory, how I remembered an apple tree and feeling sick from eating green apples. That place was also a short distance from Ted's house.

"There *was* an apple tree!" Ted blurted out, seeming surprised by my memory and by my jolting his memory. At breakfast he had mentioned that he remembered very little about his childhood.

"That's where your father's sister lived," Ted said, "in that apartment right next to us."

I thought of my father and his cousins going to his sister's apartment and drinking there and then going over to my mother's apartment.

Being contemptuous of people who drank, I can't imagine that my mother was too happy about them coming over. Her first husband, my siblings' father, sold liquor to the Indians in Flagstaff in the early forties. He was a heavy drinker and my sister, about four at the time, remembers him beating our mother until a neighbor intervened and stopped him, warning him that he would get the same if he were ever to beat her again.

He was having an affair with a teenager when my mother decided to leave. She sold his liquor bottles when he wasn't home and borrowed money from the neighbor for train fare. She took her children to Las Vegas, New Mexico, where a sister got her a job cleaning motel rooms with her. And from then on she was condemned to a life of poverty, along with her children, while her husband went on to marry the teenager and later had a filling station in Albuquerque.

A few years back, I found a census record for 1940 that lists my father. He was ten years old. He would have been about nineteen when I was conceived, and my mother would have been thirty-one. He was much too young, as she told me.

13.

When I was very young, I remember someone playing a record in the house that has stayed in my mind as the earliest song I remember hearing. What I remembered was something that sounded sort of like *woosomewerry*. For years I puzzled over what those nonsensical words, more sounds than words, could possibly mean. I felt a strong need to know what the song was, who sang it.

One day I was visiting my sister and mentioned that for years I had been trying to identify a song I heard when I was very young. I told her I had recently heard a song from the fifties that I suspected might be the song. Part of the song stirred a strong feeling within me when I heard it. It was "Blueberry Hill" by Fats Domino. Really, it was the refrain "Blueberry Hill" that stirred something within me.

When I mentioned the song, my sister nodded enthusiastically. That had been one of her records.

14.

When I was in the twelfth grade, nearing graduation, I didn't know what I was going to do after high school. There was no money for me to go to college. And I didn't know anything about scholarships or financial aid. I never even considered that any of that was possible for me.

I had a vague idea of moving to Albuquerque, living in some cheap hotel room, writing poetry, and working wherever I could get a job. But the reality was if I didn't go to college, I most likely would have been drafted and sent to Vietnam. That happened to my best friend. And one of my football teammates died in Vietnam.

One day as my senior year was coming to an end, I was in the counselor's office, where I had never been before. I had passed by it many times without giving it much thought. Maybe the counselor motioned for me to come in as I was walking by. He asked me what I planned to do after graduation. Go to college? I told him I didn't have any plans. Then he had a thought. He swiveled in his chair, bent over, and picked up a letter from out of his trash can.

"Here's a possibility," he said. "There's a minority students' program being formed at the University of New Mexico in Albuquerque. Your grades are high enough for them to consider you. If you're interested, I can set it up so that you take their test. And if you pass, they'll interview you."

Two men came to my school from Albuquerque. I took their test, they interviewed me, and soon afterward I heard that I had been accepted. It was just in time. Graduation was only a few days away.

To begin with, the program consisted of a summer of classes at the university before the start of the freshman year. The teachers who taught the classes worked for the program, and the classes were geared to help us catch up to other entering students who came from families with higher incomes and who had gone to better schools.

Simon J. Ortiz was one of those counselors. He was a Pueblo Indian from Acoma and was nine years older than me. Simon was a writer and had recently attended the International Writing Program at the University of Iowa. One of his projects as a counselor was to do a poetry publication from the students in the program. I submitted some poems, which he liked.

I had been writing poetry since the ninth grade, when a young, sexy English teacher encouraged me to write poetry. Otherwise, I don't know that I would have ever considered writing poetry. I had a friend who memorized Edgar Allan Poe's "The Raven" in the seventh grade. Every chance he got he'd start reciting it. It drove me crazy and gave me a very poor opinion of poetry. But I did like reading *Mad* magazine. A lot of the stuff in it was dumb, but usually humorous, and I was inspired to write some humorous, dumb stuff. I made a little magazine, a sort of booklet, by folding several pages of paper in half and sewing the binding with a simple stitch. I passed around each new installment to classmates. I thought of it as purely fun and the other students seemed to enjoy it.

But one day I was called into the principal's office. I saw one of my booklets on his desk and thought I was in trouble. At first, he didn't say anything. He just looked at me and then looked at the booklet. Finally, he explained that he had shown my booklet to my English teacher and she had said that what I was writing reminded her of poetry. "Poetry?" I thought, confused. The principal then said that he wanted me to meet with my teacher after class to discuss what I was writing. I was delighted. My teacher wore short dresses. She had marvelous legs. Sometimes she'd sit on her desk with one leg crossed over the other. I don't know that I ever heard anything she said as I stared at those incredible legs, so much bare skin.

I was a very shy student and had never spoken to my teacher. And to hear from the principal that she was going to meet with me after class, I was ecstatic. If she thought what I wrote was poetry, that was fine with me. When we met after class, she lent me some books of poetry and some books about poetry. I read through the books and I began writing what I imagined might be poetry because that is what my teacher wanted to see. She liked what I wrote and encouraged me to write more poetry, and I kept writing so I could spend more time with her. She was beautiful, young, sexy. That was all the inspiration I needed.

15.

Simon encouraged me to write poetry. He lived in the same dorm I lived in, and sometimes I'd drop in on him and hear him talk about what he had learned about writing when he was at Iowa. I particularly remember him talking about Charles Olson's ideas about line length, how it was a measurement of a poet's breath. The rest of my four years in college, and even afterward, Simon and I remained friends.

One afternoon a little over a year after I graduated from college, I stopped by to see Simon. Maybe he had asked me to stop by to meet some people, two young men a little older than me. One of them was the editor of *Puerto del Sol*, a literary magazine at New Mexico State University in Las Cruces. They were probably offering Simon a teaching assistantship along with being the poetry editor of *Puerto del Sol*. Simon wasn't interested and recommended me. Until then the thought of going to graduate school hadn't been anything I had considered.

I wasn't interested in academia, or in teaching, and I couldn't have imagined how I would have paid for graduate school even if I had been interested. But here was an offer out of the blue, my tuition paid for and enough money to live on—just barely. I didn't see what I had to lose. At that time, I had a job driving a truck for a company that made Indian jewelry for the tourist market.

After getting my BA in English, I hadn't had any success getting a decent job and had gone from one lousy job to another. As my senior year was coming to an end, a naval recruiter was on campus looking for students for officer's training. I was thinking I wanted a drastic change in my life, so I went for an interview and took a test, which I passed. He gave me application forms to fill out and told me to take them to the recruiting office downtown. But next to the navy's recruiting office was the coast guard's recruiting office. When I was a young teenager, I had seen an infomercial on the coast guard at a movie theater. It had made a big impression on me, and I decided to go in and chat with the recruiter. Before I knew it, I signed up as a regular recruit with the coast guard. It seemed to me a more fitting occupation for a poet. The only concern was that the coast guard had higher eye standards than any other branch of the service, but the recruiter said there was a law in Congress to lower that eye standard. He was certain that it would go through. After I had been in basic training in California for a little less than a month, I was told that the law hadn't gone through and that they would have to give me a medical discharge. I had signed up with the coast guard thinking I was going to be there for at least four years and had spent the little money I had taking a girlfriend on a trip to Chihuahua, Mexico, and gave away my few possessions. But in less than a month, I was back in Albuquerque with what was left of my pay after I bought a bus ticket from Oakland. When I got back to Albuquerque, I desperately applied for any job I saw in the newspaper, all low paying, needing some money fast. I even applied for a position as a dishwasher, but fortunately I was offered a better job as a typesetter at a small Albuquerque newspaper. The truck-driving job was my third job in a little over a year.

Going to graduate school in Las Cruces, even though the pay wasn't much, seemed to be an opportunity to break out of the rut I had gotten into. Near the end of the second semester, I went to see my grandmother who was staying with my uncle Sam, who worked for the state and had recently transferred from Santa Fe to Las Cruces. Since her husband died, my grandmother had been living with different children, mostly in the Bay Area of California, where many of her children had moved because of the job opportunities. She hadn't been in New Mexico in many years and was anxious to spend some time in her house in Chacón, where she hadn't lived since her husband died fourteen years earlier, but none of her children were able to get free to spend time with her there. She was too old, and the house was too remote, for her to be there by herself.

My grandmother whispered in my ear in Spanish, "Vamos a mi casa este verano." She wanted me to spend the summer, or part of the summer, with her in her house in Chacón. Being in her eighties, she knew that she didn't have much time left. And in fact, she died a year later.

I liked the idea. I was finding academia detrimental to my creative writing. So I gladly accepted my grandmother's offer. The academic classes had been turning my ability to write poetry into knots. For years, writing poetry had been an important part of my life. And without the poetry happening, my life seemed empty. I hoped that by getting away to Chacón for part of the summer, to the house where I was born, spending time with my grandmother, and having time to clear my head would help save me from losing my ability to write poetry—or poetry of any worth, at any rate. But this decline in my poetry hadn't just started at New Mexico State and academia. A series of lousy, low-paying jobs had started that wearing-down process.

16.

I got to Chacón in an old Chrysler New Yorker, my first car. I saw it for sale in the classified ads, and I had just enough money to buy it—$500—the money I was paid for doing a one-week poetry workshop at a school in Santa Fe for the New Mexico Arts Commission. I had never been far enough ahead financially before to afford a car. A couple years earlier I had come close to getting married. We went as far as getting blood tests and picking up the marriage license, which my girlfriend kept, but after that we didn't contact each other. I think she wised up to the fact that we would have struggled financially. And, importantly, I didn't own a car.

That had been eating away at me, not owning a car. So, without having the car inspected—I knew so little about owning a car—I turned over my small fortune and landed up with a lemon.

The Arab students I bought the car from were returning home, I think to Saudi Arabia. I imagined they laughed all the way home thinking of what a sucker I was. It didn't take long before the car stopped working. Since I had spent all my money on the car, I didn't have any money to have it repaired. Finally, I checked out a book from the library on fixing cars and even though I hadn't known anything about fixing cars before, I figured out that my starter needed to be replaced. But I didn't have the money to buy the part. Instead, I learned how to hot-wire the car using a screwdriver. I'd open the hood, apply the screwdriver to the starter, and electrical sparks would go flying. Then the car would start up, though not always right away.

I got to Chacón more than a week before my grandmother got there. Since I last saw her in Las Cruces, she had gone back to San Francisco and was dependent on someone getting free to take her to Chacón, which gave me time alone to reflect on things. In Chacón I parked the car to the side of my grandmother's house, next to a row of lilac bushes, hoping I wouldn't have to drive it for some time.

I took several books with me to read and didn't intend to do any writing. I wanted to relax, take in the environment, and let the knots that had been forming in my brain start loosening up, and hopefully get the one year of academia out of my system. Each day, I went out hiking in the mountains, reveling in what I hadn't been allowed to do when I was younger. I hiked the mountains on both sides of the valley, discovering a small lake and a place where water was gushing out of the side of the mountain. And back at the house I would sit on the porch absorbing the world around me, the views of the valley, the nature sounds, the quality of the air and the light. Gradually the knots my creativity had gotten into began to unravel.

One day when I was sitting on the porch taking in the valley, and the river flowing through it, I suddenly saw the valley as being pure white and the river, a black line—a sinuous curve across that whiteness. I felt a sudden need to draw. I didn't have any drawing materials, so I hot-wired the car. To my surprise it started up quickly. I drove about forty miles to the bookstore at New Mexico Highlands University in Las Vegas and bought a pad of drawing paper, the whitest they had, and a bottle of ink and a crow quill pen. I hurried back to Chacón and made a couple drawings of the mountains as seen from the porch. From then on, I took my drawing materials with me when I went out walking and drew old farm equipment, an old shack, and pine trees; in the house, I drew lilacs I had put in a glass and views of different parts of the kitchen. The drawing aided in clearing out my brain. When I returned to New Mexico State for the fall semester, the poetry came effortlessly, was more expressive. And I continued to draw, a sort of meditation.

17.

After my grandmother arrived in Chacón, before relatives from California started arriving and I left, we spent some time alone. It was the summer, but my grandmother was always cold. She had gotten accustomed to the warmer weather of California, but also, she was much older than when she last lived in Chacón, and at eight-thousand-plus feet elevation, there were summer days that were chilly and the nights could get cold. My grandmother would spend a great deal of the time sitting by the woodstove, which I kept going all the time. She wore a housecoat and slippers. Sometimes she would shuffle outside looking for estafiate to make a tea for her ailments. She never had to go very far to find estafiate, not even as far as the ojito, the spring where we got our water.

I sometimes tried to ask my grandmother about the past: what was it like in the old days, where did our ancestors come from before they crossed over the Sangre de Cristo Mountains to settle the east side? Having lived in California for a long time, my grandmother could understand English much better. I heard from an aunt that my grandmother had become addicted to soap operas. Now she'd use a word or two of English. But our conversations were still awkward though better than they had been in the past. To my questions, my grandmother would say, "Era antes"—*It was before*. And when I'd press her more, she'd say, "Todo era too pretty." It was too beautiful, too wonderful, she'd mean, when there were more people there.

While we were still in Chacón by ourselves, with only a visit from her son William, who lived across the river, we learned from him that the face of Jesus was being seen on the wall of a small building next to the church in Holman (originally called Agua Negra). My grandmother wanted to see this apparition so I took her. Surprisingly, my car performed well for this trip, a miracle of sorts. I didn't see the face of Jesus, and as far I could tell, neither did my grandmother.

18.

At my brother Ted's fiftieth wedding anniversary, copies of a photograph were given out. It's a copy of a black-and-white photograph and has a few creases after many years of being handled. One crease partly obliterates half of my brother Albert's nose and half of his mouth. Otherwise, the faces of the rest of the attendees at this party have remained unscathed. A few times over the years, I had heard of a photograph of a party my siblings attended when they were children, and, oh, by the way, "You're in the picture."

I'm the youngest of the twenty children gathered to have their photograph taken and look like I'm around two or three years old. Being the smallest of the children, I must have been told to stand in the front row, where the youngest children are in addition to the birthday boy, whom I'm standing next to and who is an older child. He is directly in front of his birthday cake and is looking at the camera, just barely smiling. He is wearing a suit jacket (every other child is dressed casually), and what looks like a small flower is pinned to his jacket lapel. One hand is resting flat on the edge of the table to the side of the

cake. The other hand, at the other side of the cake, is raised with three
fingers pressing so tightly against the edge of the table that his fingers
are bent inward. His father was the high school music teacher, and he
has the self-assured, smug look of one of the more well-to-do in an
economically poor community.

I have a bewildered or dazed look and am wearing what looks like
a frock, a shirt that's too large for me. At that time my mother worked
cleaning the house of an Anglo family in new town. They would some-
times give her clothes their children had outgrown, which I often
wore. I suspect that's where that shirt came from.

In the top row where the tallest children are, my sister, Sara, stands
next to my two brothers. There is another boy in the top row with
a wide smile who is a little taller than my sister, otherwise she's the
tallest child in the picture, which is curious to see because I've always
known her to be short, a little under five feet. In the photo she's a cou-
ple of inches taller than Albert, who eventually got to be close to six
feet tall. Next to Albert in the picture is my oldest brother, Ted, who is
two years younger than Sara and a year older than Albert. Looking at
the photograph I can fully understand why I have such few memories
of my siblings when I was growing up. They were already well on their
way with their lives, seven to ten years older than me, while I was still
hardly more than a baby. What could my siblings have had in common
with me? Nothing other than that we lived in the same house and had
the same mother.

19.

I have a wallet-size school photo of me when I was in kindergarten. I'm
wearing a cowboy-style shirt that came from that Anglo family who
gave my mother clothes. I have a big smile in that photograph, a smile
I wasn't to repeat in any other photograph even up through the end of
high school. The big smile gave way to a subdued or sullen look.

I have memories of various fights throughout elementary school,
beginning with the first day of school. When I was in the third grade,
one bully continually started fights with me. I fought back even though
he was stronger than me and I got the worst of it. One day, in exas-

peration that I kept fighting back, the bully said, "Why don't you ever speak Spanish?" I didn't know what to answer.

My mother spoke Spanish, my siblings spoke Spanish, all my relatives spoke Spanish, many of the children in my elementary school spoke Spanish, but I didn't. I felt a bit of a panic when he asked me the question. It was the panic I felt when an uncle would pierce me with his harsh stare when he'd address me in Spanish and I'd respond in English. I understood what was said to me in Spanish, but if I tried to speak in Spanish, my mind would freeze up or the Spanish words would get jumbled up.

After the bully asked me that question, he never picked on me again. I think he finally realized it was pointless. I was going to continue fighting, I was never going to give in to him, and I was never going to say a word in Spanish. Not long afterward, I heard that he had been sent to a reform school. But certainly not because he had been fighting with me. As far as I could see, he had free reign on the playground to do whatever he wanted to me. No one ever interfered.

In another school photograph about two years later, I'm wearing a leather Western-style jacket that was also a hand-me-down from that Anglo family. There's a patch of paint in the top corner of a shoulder where I accidentally brushed against a newly painted wall at school. It still irks me to see that paint stain.

I was given those early school photos, and others, when I finished the sixth grade and was moving on to junior high. I believe my elementary school records were being discarded, but the small yearly photos, with staple marks where they had been attached to my records, were given to me. My mother had similar photos. They were samples of the photos taken at the beginning of the school year, which students took home with the expectation that a set of photos would be ordered.

20.

Recently I was on the internet looking for information on a childhood friend, Paulajean Segura, whom I had lost contact with by the time I was eight. My interest was sparked because her sister had been in my bookstore and said Paulajean had died in California some years back. She, Paulajean, and their mother had moved there together, but after losing Paulajean and her mother, she decided to return to New Mexico.

I found very little about Paulajean on the internet, but there was one newspaper article that caught my eye. The newspaper was the *Las Vegas Daily Optic*, the local paper. The article was about a birthday party for Paulajean, and I was surprised to see that my name came up as one of the children in attendance. Unfortunately, when the article was digitized portions of the text became nothing but meaningless letters, numbers, and characters. I couldn't find a date because so much of the article was unreadable. And then I suddenly made a connection between the birthday party and an early memory.

The memory is like a remembered dream. I'm going to a birthday party, but all I have to give as a gift is a dime. I remember wondering what I could do to improve the gift. My mother had a small bottle of mercury. I don't know why she had it since mercury's a poison. Maybe people weren't so aware of that back then. I've read that in the 1800s it was used in medicines—probably killing more people than it cured. I got the bottle and poured some drops in my palm. The mercury separated into silver balls of different sizes. It wasn't the first time I had put some mercury in my hands. I liked tilting my palm back and forth and seeing the silvery balls roll around. I rubbed the mercury over the dime, getting it as shiny as I could. The new-looking dime seemed to me like a more fitting gift.

I had a vague memory of holding the dime while standing on the sidewalk alongside South Pacific Avenue, as if waiting for something to happen. But after seeing the article, I realized I was standing in front of Paulajean's house, hesitating before going to the party. I don't remember anything about that party except for a vague memory of a room with children.

21.

My mother gave me a dime for me to spend however I wanted. It was something she seldom was able to do. I went to Dick's store feeling prosperous. But before going into the store, I decided to hang upside down on the small cylindrical metal railing that ran along the cement steps leading up to the store. The store was on a hillside rising up sharply from South Pacific. Without thinking that I had the dime in my shirt pocket, I hung upside down, and then I saw the dime fall into the gray, ash-covered ground to the side of the walkway. It was where Dick dumped the ashes from his potbelly stove. It was an accumulation of years. I hurriedly got off the bar and frantically searched through the ashes. I dug and dug but the dime had vanished.

When I'm visiting Las Vegas, I'll sometimes drive past the small building, long abandoned, where Dick's store once was. I'll cast a glance at it, at the steps leading up to it, and to the general area where the dime was lost, and I'll recall once again that deep sense of loss, that small fortune gone.

22.

When my wife and I arrived in Las Vegas to attend Ted's wedding anniversary, we were early so I slowly drove around the neighborhood where I had lived, at three different places, from when I was about four until I graduated from high school and left for college in Albuquerque. Since I graduated from high school, I've only returned to Las Vegas for short visits and those have gotten less frequent since my mother passed away.

"You like driving through here," my wife said with a slight smile as I drove slowly, looking intently at what I saw, and too there was a hint of tiredness in her voice: *Oh no, not this drive again!* I didn't explain that when I drove through the old neighborhood it seemed totally different to me each time. But no matter the difference, I still felt a connection, though tenuous. It intrigues me, this difference, but also leaves me somewhat disconcerted by how different my experiences always are as I drive through my old neighborhood. And so I fail to get a grasp of anything tangible. Everything I'm experiencing is so removed, so remote, from my current life and from how my life has been for such a long time. What am I expecting to discover, to experience? There are clues everywhere hinting at what? The child I was, the life I lived? But by the end of my drive around the neighborhood, nothing is revealed. I'm left with a disquieting feeling and a sense of sadness. That past that once was so full of life is not even a shell of its former self. It's more like an accumulation of dust, the dust of all the years that have gone by. And beneath those layers of dust, I suspect there's nothing, though

I keep hoping for something. I guess by taking that drive, I partly hope to reduce the distance of that long-ago time and to grasp some of the emotions I felt then, because certain emotions do begin to stir as I slowly drive around the neighborhood, but then it's like something always blocks those emotions. The drive always ends too soon and any revelatory feelings I was beginning to experience, slight inklings anyway, suddenly vanish.

I once walked around the neighborhood. That was better than driving. I paused often, as if expecting something to occur, as if the past could suddenly appear strolling down a dirt driveway from the back of a house or be found standing in a porch. Nothing remains of a house my family rented two rooms in when I was eight and nine years old except the foundation. Did it burn down? I walked past the junior high I attended and the elementary school. Also, nothing there but foundations. As with driving, the walk ended too soon, leaving me with the hope that maybe someday something will be revealed, something of who I was, something I crave to experience again through this wall of time that becomes as solid as granite the closer I approach it.

Along my walk, a small group of children approached me cautiously but smiling. Did they recognize me?

ACKNOWLEDGMENTS

SOME POEMS IN THIS COLLECTION were originally published in *During the Growing Season* (The Maguey Press, 1978); *Celso* (Quinto Sol Publications, 1980); *Agua Negra* (Ahsahta Press, 1981); *Celso*, a later edition (Arte Público Press, 1985); *Desert Nights*, a chapbook (Fishdrum, 1989); *Going Home Away Indian* (Ahsahta Press, 1990; a second, limited edition was published in 2010); and *San Fernandez Beat* (Alexander Street Press, 1992). *During the Growing Season, Celso*, and *Agua Negra* were recently revised (unpublished), and many of those poems are in this collection.

Poems in this collection appeared in the following anthologies and literary magazines:

Spectrum, 1975

Puerto del Sol, 1976

sou'wester, 1976

Beloit Poetry Journal, Winter 1976–77

South Dakota Review, Winter 1976–77

The Indian Rio Grande: Recent Poems from 3 Cultures, San Marcos Press, 1977

San Marcos Review, 1977

Southwest: A Contemporary Anthology, 1977

Puerto del Sol: New Mexico Anthology Issue, 1978

San Marcos Review, 1978

plumbers ink: A Journal of Contemporary Poetry, 1979

Revista Chicano-Riqueña, 1979

Dacotah Territory, 1980

Hispanics in the United States: An Anthology of Creative Literature, Bilingual
   Review Press, 1980

Berkeley Poetry Review, 1981

Bilingual Review, 1982

A Decade of Hispanic Literature: An Anniversary Anthology, Arte Público
   Press, 1982

Puerto del Sol, 1982

Puerto del Sol, 1983

Crossing the River: Poets of the Western United States, Permanent Press, 1987

Voces: An Anthology of Nuevo Mexicano Writers, University of New Mexico
   Press, 1987

Sonora Review, 1988

South Dakota Review, 1989

Northwest Review, 1990

Sotto il Quinto Sole: Antologia di poeti chicani, Passigli Editori, 1990

Bilingual Review, 1992

New Mexico Poetry Renaissance, Red Crane Books, 1994

Recent Chicano Poetry / Neueste Chicano-Lyric, Bamberg, 1994

yefief, 1994

L'Ozio, 1995

Paper Dance: 55 Latino Poets, Persea Books, 1995

¡Saludos! Poemas de Nuevo Mexico / Poems of New Mexico, Pennywhistle
   Press, 1995

*The Ahsahta Anthology: Modern and Contemporary Poetry of the American
   West*, Ahsahta Press, 1996

Fish Drum Magazine, 1998

The Floating Borderlands: Twenty-Five Years of U.S. Hispanic Literature,
   University of Washington Press, 1998

Real Things: An Anthology of Popular Culture in American Poetry, Indiana
   University Press, 1999

Poesia, 2000

Pinto di Vista, 2001

Santa Fe Literary Review, 2007

I Wanna Be Loved by You: Poems on Marilyn Monroe, Milk & Cake Press,
   2022

Latino Poetry: A New Anthology, Library of America, 2024

ABOUT THE AUTHOR

Leo Romero was born in Chacón, New Mexico, in 1950. He has a master of arts in English from New Mexico State University. In the 1970s he worked for the Social Security Administration. In the '80s he worked at Los Alamos National Laboratory. Since 1988, Leo's been a bookseller in Santa Fe, New Mexico. He has sold two bookstores at different times, retiring briefly each time (two years and then one and a half years). His current bookstore is Books of Interest, which his wife, Elizabeth, runs with him after working for several years as a journalist. Besides poetry, Leo has also published a book of short fiction, *Rita & Los Angeles* (Bilingual Press, 1995). In 1985 a play, *I Am Celso*, was adapted from poems in *Celso* and *Agua Negra* by the Seattle Group Theatre Company and toured around the country. Leo was awarded a National Endowment for the Arts fellowship for poetry, is a Pushcart Prize winner, and was a Helene Wurlitzer Foundation resident.